UNCOVERING
What RELIGION
Has to HIDE

Colombia para Cristo video introduction

Watch the *La Montaña* trailer, a film based on a true Stendal event

UNCOVERING What RELIGION Has to HIDE

The Testimony of Simon Peter

Russell M. Stendal

Visit Russell's website: www.cpcsociety.ca

Uncovering What Religion Has to Hide – Russell M. Stendal

Copyright © 2015

First edition published 2015

Cover Design: Amber Burger

Cover Photography: Helen Hotson/Shutterstock

Editors: Sheila Wilkinson, Ruth Zetek

Printed in the United States of America

By Aneko Press – *Our Readers Matter*™

www.anekopress.com

Aneko Press, Life Sentence Publishing, and our logos are trademarks of Life Sentence Publishing, Inc.
203 E. Birch Street
P.O. Box 652
Abbotsford, WI 54405

RELIGION / Christian Church / General

Paperback ISBN: 978-1-62245-281-1

Ebook ISBN: 978-1-62245-282-8

10 9 8 7 6 5 4 3 2 1

Available wherever books are sold.

Share this book on Facebook:

Contents

CHAPTER 1

Prepare the Way

Where does your theology come from? Some people form their theology from the law of Moses. Scripture states that God's law is the truth and his commandments are eternal (Psalm 119:98, 142). However, it also tells us that all men have sinned and none are righteous (Romans 3:10, 23). The only one who could fulfill the law is the Lord Jesus Christ (Matthew 5:17). If we go back and attempt to fulfill the law in our own strength, we return to legalism. Only Jesus Christ could fulfill the law. The letter kills; the Spirit of God brings forth life (2 Corinthians 3:6).

Other people concentrate on the Pauline epistles of the New Testament. Some who focus on grace instead of the law define grace as "unmerited favor." When they take this to an extreme, however, they end up proportionately focusing on what Christ has done and largely ignore a Christian's need to follow the Lord Jesus Christ. This can be taken as permission for licentiousness or other sins by those who think the law no longer applies. Knowing they have prayed a "sinner's prayer," they assume they are covered. They believe in the death and resurrection of Jesus Christ, they congregate in a church, and they pay their tithes, so they believe this grace must cover them no matter what they do.

But unmerited favor is only a secondary definition of grace. The primary definition of grace is the power of God to change and transform us, linking us to the presence of God. And those who are led by the Spirit of God are not under the law (Galatians 5:18).

Therefore, the center of the Scriptures, the center of the plan of God, the center of everything, is the Lord Jesus. If we speak of the law, we must do this in the context of who the Lord Jesus really is, what he has done, and what he will do for us. If we speak of grace, it cannot be separated from the Lord Jesus. His name is Jesus, but he also has another name, and that other name is Christ. Jesus means "savior" (the author of salvation). Christ means "anointing" or "the anointed one."

Isaiah 10:27 refers to an anointing that will destroy the yoke, an anointing that breaks and dissolves the heavy yoke of religion. The Lord Jesus is the Anointed One who has that anointing. He is the only one who has it. No one else has been able to live a life that is pleasing to the Father. Jesus came to redeem us. He overcame death and then sent the Holy Spirit so we can walk in his victory.

A great controversy arose in the church over one thousand years ago as to who sent the Holy Spirit. Did the Holy Spirit proceed from the Father or from the Son? The Father and the Son, however, are of one accord. Their desire is to send the Holy Spirit to bond us with them. The Lord Jesus as the only mediator of the New Covenant, sends his Spirit with the goal that we can be cleansed by the power of God and come to know the Father.

Mark 1

1 *The beginning of the gospel of Jesus, the Christ,*
Son of God,

Many preach a gospel (which they define as "good news") that is different from what is written here. This gospel in Mark 1 speaks of the Son of God and of a kingdom that is different from the kingdoms of men. The word *gospel* was already in use in the Roman Empire when Jesus entered the scene. *Gospel* or *good news* was used on special occasions when there was a change of kings or kingdoms. *King* and *kingdom* have the same root word in Greek. The kingdom is everything under the authority of the king. This includes people and territory.

When a new king came on the scene (after the old king died or was killed), with a subsequent change in government, the "gospel" was the proclamation of this important change. Since humans are corrupted by power, the old pagan king had most likely become corrupt. The death of the old tyrant and the rise of the new king was always "good news" to the people. Unlike today, when most countries have elections every four years, at that time it could take thirty, forty, or even fifty years for the old despot to die. Imagine having to put up with that.

When at last the old Caesar was dead or deposed, heralds went forth under armed escort into every corner of the empire. They blew the trumpets and proclaimed that there was a new king. When the proclamation or gospel ("good news") of the new king was announced, everyone had to make a choice. They either had to kneel and swear allegiance to Caesar as lord and worship the new king (the Romans thought that Caesar was God), or the Roman soldiers immediately dealt with them. Many Christians were killed in this way by the Romans because they refused to worship Caesar as God.

The greeting among the early Christians was "Jesus is Lord." The reply was "Yes, he is Lord indeed!" This is the beginning of the gospel. This is the gospel that declares that the Lord Jesus is our new king. We may accept him or reject him, but he is the sovereign King. The word *gospel* does not just mean "good news," however. It means we have a new king and do not have to serve Satan, the old despot, any longer.

This gospel is recorded, or written down, by John Mark. Mark was a young boy on the night that Jesus was betrayed prior to the crucifixion. Remember that all the disciples fled, but there was a young lad clothed in a sheet nearby. The Roman soldiers grabbed the sheet and the boy fled, naked (Mark 14:50-52).

Peter called Mark his son (1 Peter 5:13), and it is very likely that this writing is the gospel related by Peter and written down by Mark. Peter was an uneducated fisherman when Jesus called him. Another confirmation of this is that in the early church, as the early fathers were establishing the canon of the sixty-six books of the Bible, and separating them from spurious books, one of the key criteria was that the true books of the New Testament had to be written, dictated, or authorized by the apostles who had received their commission directly from the Lord Jesus. Mark is never mentioned as an apostle like Peter or Paul or John, so we are led to believe that Peter authorized this gospel.

After he denied the Lord three times before the rooster crowed twice, Peter became very humble (Mark 14:72; John 21:15-19). Peter may have not wanted to sign his name to the book. He wanted God to get all the glory.

1 *The beginning of the gospel of Jesus, the Christ, Son of God,*

Imagine Simon Peter dictating this and young John Mark writing it down.

2 *as it is written in the prophets, Behold, I send my messenger before thy face, who shall prepare thy way before thee.*

3 *The voice of one crying in the wilderness, Prepare ye the way of the Lord; make his paths straight.*

He is referring to Isaiah:

Isaiah 40

3 *The voice of him that cries in the wilderness,*

*Prepare ye the way of the LORD; make straight in
the desert a highway for our God.*

*4 Every valley shall be exalted, and every mountain
and hill shall be made low; and the crooked shall be
made straight, and the rough places made plain:*

*5 And the glory of the LORD shall be manifested,
and all flesh shall see it together, for the mouth of
the LORD has spoken it.*

*6 The voice that said, Cry. And I said, What shall I
cry? All flesh is grass, and all the mercy thereof is as
the open flower of the field:*

*7 The grass withers, the flower fades because the
spirit of the LORD blows upon it; surely the people
is grass.*

*8 The grass withers, the open flower fades; but the
word of our God shall stand for ever.*

What does this mean?

When we live here on earth in the flesh, we are like grass
that lasts for a very short time. Even when we are born the second
time and blossom with gifts from God, and the Holy Spirit
flourishes in our being, this life is very transitory. The purpose
of our lives is to produce the fruit of righteousness, the mature
character of God in our being. This fruit of the Holy Spirit will
endure forever. Later, Peter quotes Isaiah again:

1 Peter 1

*23 being born again, not of corruptible seed, but of
incorruptible, by the word of God, which lives and
abides for ever.*

24 For all flesh is as grass, and all the glory of man

as the flower of grass. The grass withers, and its flower falls away,

25 but the word of the Lord endures for ever. And this is the word which by the gospel is preached unto you.

It is clear that Peter, inspired by the Holy Spirit, has a different concept of the gospel from what is prevalent in many of our churches with modern-day Laodiceans.

Mark 1

4 John baptized in the wilderness and preached the baptism of repentance for remission of sins.

The Greek literally says, "baptism *into* repentance."

Under the law, if someone became unclean, they had to be washed with water. There were many ways to become unclean. John was preaching that the entire nation was unclean. Those who sought the baptism of John were publicly recognizing that they were unclean and, therefore, not acceptable to God.

Repentance is different from crocodile tears. Repentance means a one-hundred-and-eighty-degree reversal. If we are heading downhill, we must turn around and head uphill. If we are heading south, we must turn and head north. If we are going our own way and seeking to satisfy our own desires, we must turn and go God's way and seek to satisfy his desires. God offers us a time and place to repent. If we do not respond, we have no guarantee we will have the same opportunity later.

John's ministry only lasted five or six months until Jesus came on the scene. He baptized the Jewish people into repentance. He was commissioned to immerse them into repentance, and he used water as a symbol. Later, in Luke chapter 7, we see that those who received the baptism of John *justified God* and were able to understand the plan and purpose of God in Jesus

Christ. Those who refused the baptism of John rejected the counsel of God against themselves.

Those who refused to repent were unable to understand the gospel of Jesus Christ. They remained clueless. They desired a messiah who would implement a grand kingdom and restore even more than the glory of Solomon. When Jesus said that his kingdom is not of this world, some were very disillusioned. Jesus came to announce a different kingdom and he started by planting a word. Scripture states that the word goes forth we know not how, first the blade, then the ear, and finally the fullness of the fruit (Mark 4:28). It is the fruit that will remain.

John was sent to prepare the way, and he did this by preaching repentance and baptizing those who responded to his message. Later, when Jesus was about to leave, he told his disciples that they were clean, not because of the baptism of John, but because of the word that he had given them (John 15:3). True cleanness comes from hearkening unto the word of the Lord and hearing the voice of the Lord. When we receive his word by faith, he provides the grace to bring his word forth in us as obedient reality.

> 5 *And there went out unto him all the land of Judaea and those of Jerusalem and were all baptized of him in the river Jordan, confessing their sins.*

These people desired to have a new beginning with God, so God would blot out their past and allow them to start over. *Jordan* means "to flow down," and in our natural state, all of us are flowing down, headed for death and decay. John submerged them in water as a symbol of death to all their own sins and ambitions, so they could seek the kingdom of God.

> 6 *John was clothed with camel's hair and with a girdle of a skin about his loins; and he ate locusts and wild honey*

7 and preached, saying, There comes one mightier than I after me, the latchet of whose shoes I am not worthy to stoop down and unloose.

8 I indeed have baptized you with water, but he shall baptize you with the Holy Spirit.

The maximum that human ministry can accomplish is to baptize someone in water, but the water is only a symbol. Human ministry cannot submerge anyone into the Holy Spirit unless they are operating in union with Jesus. Many come up out of the water as corrupt as they were before. No miraculous change has taken place. They come out of the water, wet, and possibly a bit cleaner on the surface. But if the Lord Jesus does not effect a work deep within and bring us to genuine repentance and baptize us (immerse us) into the Holy Spirit, we will not enter the kingdom of heaven. Our only hope is to trust him.

John came in the spirit and power of Elijah (Malachi 4:5; Luke 1:17) in at least a partial fulfillment of Malachi 4. At the first coming, not too many Jews were reconciled to God, and the land was completely destroyed by AD 70. However, at that time most were not aware that the Lord would come twice.

Now, another ministry like John the Baptist's and Elijah's is calling everyone to repentance prior to the second coming of the Lord. This time the ministry is not a single individual. God is raising up many people in many lands to blow the trumpet and announce this "gospel of the kingdom" that shall be preached to the ends of the earth. Then the end shall come (Matthew 24:14). God is sending his messengers to prepare the way for the second coming.

6 John was clothed with camel's hair

The camel was an unclean animal, so this was not clothing fit for a priest. John was a descendant of Aaron, born of Elizabeth, the cousin of Mary; and his father, Zacharias, was one who had a turn at being the high priest (Luke 1:5-17). John, however, did not dress like a priest and did not minister in the temple like his father. He dressed like Elijah and ministered in the desert. A camel could handle the desert and go for long periods of time without food or drink.

God promises to prepare his people in the desert. This can be a literal desert or a spiritual desert. In order to qualify for the fullness of the kingdom of God, the people must go through the desert. God also places ministry in the desert, and the ministry that God places in the desert (or wilderness) is like that of the prophets (Revelation 12:6).

The prophets wore the mantle of camel's hair as one of the signs that this was not an easy way. It was hard on the flesh. This path that follows the will of God is in the midst of much difficulty. John the Baptist did not do signs and wonders. But he had a powerful message, and the people left the comfort of the towns and cities to go out to the desert to see what was going on with him at the Jordan River. Compare this to many preachers today.

John, and later Jesus, led multitudes in the desert where there was nothing, not even any food. If John had sought his own comfort, he would have been a priest back at the temple. He could have possibly been the high priest, but here he was, dressed in camel's hair in the desert.

6 and with a girdle of a skin about his loins;

We imagine that this was a belt. No, it was his underwear! And over the top was his mantle of camel's hair. He was a rustic individual. The history of the girdle of skin (or leather) goes all the way back to Adam and Eve. After they got into trouble and knew they were naked, God was not impressed with their improvised clothing made of fig leaves (it has been said that this was man's first attempt at religion).

God covered their nakedness with leather girdles. And for this, something had to die. In order to obtain a leather girdle, blood had to be shed. And later, the Israelites were not allowed to kill an animal whenever or wherever they pleased. The killing had to be part of the blood covenant with God and according to his orders. Scripture states that the life is in the blood and without the shedding of blood there is no remission (of sin). This was all designed to point to the supreme sacrifice that would be made by Jesus Christ. John had announced this: *Behold the Lamb of God, who takes away the sin of the world* (John 1:29).

So John had his intimate parts covered with a girdle of skin as a reminder that he was in a blood covenant with God. The law requires an eye for an eye, a tooth for a tooth, and a life for a life (Exodus 21:23-24). We must see things from the Lord's perspective and not from our own. He is our redeemer and our avenger, and we are not to take the law into our own hands. David summed it up like this: *For with thee is the fountain of life; in thy light shall we see light* (Psalm 36:9).

John demonstrated understanding of the covenant. We must do God's will and not our own. We are to live his life and not our own. We are to decrease and he is to increase. The city of the religion of men was not a proper starting place. The "covering" of men was not the covering of John the Baptist. An ordination certificate from the priests at Jerusalem did not cover him. He did not have a credential declaring that he was the son of the high priest. John did not even wear the robes of a priest.

His camel's hair covering was unclean in the eyes of religious men, but he was covered directly by God. When John came on the scene, Israel had been about four hundred years without a prophetic voice from God. John came emulating the prophet Elijah who had last been seen many hundreds of years before.

6 *and he ate locusts and wild honey*

In ancient Israel, several serious problems could happen. One was if a foreign army came through and trashed everything; but another was when locusts showed up. Clouds of them could descend, and millions of locusts would eat every green thing. Sometimes the resulting famine would last for years, and even decades. Sometimes the people had to leave the land due to the magnitude of the famine. Abraham experienced this, as did Jacob and his sons (Genesis 12:10; 45:16-28). Ruth and Naomi had to flee to the land of Moab (Ruth 1:1). Many times God's people had a worse time with the locusts than with enemies who wielded swords.

In Revelation chapter 9, the locusts are a symbol of enemy demonic forces. When the fifth trumpet is blown, a horde of locusts comes out of the pit to attack and sting all men who do not have the seal of God on their foreheads.

The locusts that were the terror of Israel were lunch for John the Baptist. Everyone else was afraid of the locusts (due to the famine that could ensue), but for John it was the other way around. For him the locusts were a blessing!

Those who live to feed their flesh on the "grass" of the Word of God, as if they were cattle in a pasture, fear the coming of the locusts; they fear that the enemy forces will take away all their earthly goods. But others live like John the Baptist under a different type of covering and are not trying to please their flesh. They seek to please the Lord and to serve the people of God. They understand that all things work together for good for those that love the Lord and are called according to his purpose (Romans 8:28). For these people, when the demons show up, they only serve to further the purposes of God that are hidden to the natural man.

Brethren, this is extremely important to understand. The Devil is not our most serious problem. Why do you think the Lord has allowed all these devils to roam loose for such a long period of time? Why has he not put them on ice? He will do so at the proper time. For now, however, they fulfill a useful purpose.

Even after the Devil is locked up for one thousand years, God still plans to let him loose again for a short period of time (Revelation 20:7).

Why?

He does this is to make sure that those who want to live according to their own desires, do their own thing, and foment their own selfishness and arrogance will have to reckon with the possibility of "locusts." To fall into the hands of the Devil is serious. Here in Colombia, it is relatively easy to fall into the hands of bandits or guerrillas or corrupt officials and get stung by the locusts (when all the earthly money and things that you have stored up get taken from you).

John the Baptist came to prepare the way for those who desire to serve the Lord. This is a way where even a fool will not get lost (Isaiah 35:8). This is a highway of holiness where no demon can prosper. This is a way where we do not lose our hard-earned investments to the Enemy, because we have learned to invest in heavenly treasure that is beyond his reach. This is a way where the tables turn, and we are not the food and the prey of the Enemy. Rather, the Enemy is our food and our prey!

This is the gospel according to John the Baptist and according to Simon Peter from the perspective of God.

Here is another perspective of the gospel:

The Lord Jesus described a wedding supper. The invited guests, for the most part, did not come. They were busy inspecting land to enlarge their private kingdoms. They were trying out new yokes of oxen to see how much they could "evangelize" in the flesh. They had no time to go to the great feast of the Lord (Luke 14:18-24).

In another parable, the servants were to go to the highways and gather everyone, good and bad, and bring them to the wedding feast. But one guy was thrown out of the wedding feast because he was not wearing the proper attire (Matthew 22:1-14).

What is the Lord saying?

If we submit to his authority and do his will, we will come under his covering. In Revelation 19:8, the white robes of fine linen are the righteousness of the saints. All we have to do is eat the clean food that the Lord provides, for man shall not live by bread alone but by every word that proceeds from the mouth of God (Matthew 4:4).

Revelation 19

9 And he said unto me, Write, Blessed are those who are called unto the marriage supper of the Lamb. And he said unto me, These are the true words of God.

This is a call to feed upon the true words of God. If we receive the covering that he provides, and if we eat the food that he supplies, he will take care of everything else. With these two things, we will be able to walk through hordes of demons, and they will not be able to cause us any eternal damage. They can only destroy the things of this world, and the kingdom of God is not of this world (John 18:36).

Some confusion arises here because the word translated *world* is *cosmos* in the Greek. This refers primarily to the system or the manner of doing things. For the meek shall inherit the earth (Matthew 5:5). God is going to put his government upon the earth. He will not do this by taking over the White House or the Palace of Nariño or the Vatican or the World Court or the United Nations. No, the Scripture is very clear: All of the kingdoms of this world will crumble (Daniel 2:31-45; Revelation 11:15). God's kingdom begins with a different way of doing things – his way, as he transforms hearts one by one. At the proper time, all will be revealed.

Luke 17

20 *And when he was asked of the Pharisees when the kingdom of God should come, he answered them and said, The kingdom of God does not come with observation;*

21 *neither shall they say, Behold it here! or, Behold it there! for, behold, the kingdom of God is within you.*

22 *And he said unto the disciples, The days will come when ye shall desire to see one of the days of the Son of man, and ye shall not see it.*

23 *And they shall say to you, Behold it here, or, Behold it there; do not go, nor follow them.*

24 *For as the lightning, which shines from the region under heaven, shines in that which is under heaven; so also shall the Son of man be in his day.*

In what day?

In the day of the Lord which is even now at our very door.

Over the long history of the church, many have made, and are still making, tragic mistakes as they attempt to take over the kingdoms of this world.

John the Baptist did not even attempt to take over the government of the temple in Jerusalem when he could have been the heir of the high priest. He lived in the desert and ate locusts and wild honey.

He did not eat processed honey. He ate his honey with all the natural ingredients. Honey is a symbol of the Word of God. The Old Testament warns about not eating too much honey (Proverbs 25:16), because under law and without the Spirit of God, the natural man cannot digest very much of the Word of God without getting indigestion. John the Baptist, however, and the people of God who have learned to walk in the desert can live on "honey." They can absorb great quantities of the unadulterated Word of God that can flow and flow and flow – the Word of God that has not been processed by theologians or denominations or Bible institutes. God has administered it directly. This was the diet of John the Baptist as he also munched on a few "locusts" from time to time.

Mark 1

6 *he ate locusts and wild honey*

7 *and preached, saying, There comes one mightier than I after me, the latchet of whose shoes I am not worthy to stoop down and unloose.*

In the desert, the shoes are a symbol of preparation. Traveling over hot sand and razor-sharp rocks was impossible without shoes. People could go barefoot in the farms and towns and villages but not in the desert. Moses had to take off his shoes at the burning bush (Exodus 3:5). His preparation at the house of Pharaoh had to be left behind. He had to forget what he learned there in order to lead the children of Israel out of Egypt and towards the Promised Land. Joshua also had to remove his shoes when he met with the Prince of the Lord's host (Joshua 5:15). Even the preparation in the wilderness by Joshua's great mentor, Moses, had to be left behind when he entered the Promised Land and came into the direct presence of the Prince of the Lord's host.

Jesus had a different preparation; Jesus had "shoes" that even John the Baptist was not worthy to stoop down and unloose. John was not qualified to touch Jesus' shoes even from an attitude of humility and worship. The Lord Jesus had a special preparation and formation.

Who are we to modify this and say that we can do things in a different manner? Who are we to set a curriculum of so many weeks or months or years of training and then supposedly ordain "ministers" of the gospel? Jesus was ordained by God and approved by God. He had no human credentials. He had no certificate from Herod or from the Sanhedrin or from the high priest. At the Last Supper, Jesus said, *Verily, verily, I say unto you, He that receives whomsoever I send receives me, and he that receives me receives him that sent me* (John 13:20).

When Saul of Tarsus was persecuting the believers, he went forth with letters of authorization from the high priest and from the "authorities" in Jerusalem. After the Lord Jesus captured him, his letter of recommendation was his life and the lives of the people who had been transformed by the power of God under his ministry (2 Corinthians 3:1-3). John the Baptist had made reference to that transforming power.

> 8 *I indeed have baptized you with* [Gr. "into"]
> *water, but he shall baptize you with the Holy Spirit.*

To baptize is to immerse. John immersed people into water but made it clear to the people that Jesus would immerse them into the Holy Spirit, into a new life, into a new nature with new desires. Many years later, people who had received the baptism of John had not yet received the baptism into the Holy Spirit (Acts 18:24-19:7).

> 9 *And it came to pass in those days that Jesus came from Nazareth a city of Galilee and was baptized of John in the Jordan.*
>
> 10 *And as soon as he was come out of the water, John saw the heavens opened and the Spirit like a dove descending and resting upon him;*
>
> 11 *and there came a voice from heaven, saying, Thou art my dear Son, in whom I delight.*

Scripture tells us that Jesus was about thirty years of age when this took place (Luke 3:21-23). Under the law, a Levite had to be at least thirty years old to be in the ministry. Seven times this requirement is stated in the book of Numbers. According to Jewish custom, the Levite could also come into the fullness of the inheritance of his father at age thirty.

Even a baby can receive a gift such as the earnest or down payment of the Spirit with measure. Paul writes about the earnest of the Spirit (Ephesians 1:13-14). What Jesus received at the Jordan River was not the earnest; he received the fullness of the Spirit without measure. Note that his Father was delighted with him even before he began his ministry. God will not give this type of anointing to anyone who is still seeking to promote his own life and his own kingdom. God will not give this anointing to anyone whom he does not expressly send (John 3:34).

Jesus could have been an excellent Messiah at age twelve, but he would not have saved us. In order to save us, he had to completely fulfill the plan of God. God's plan is that no one can have a ministry in fullness without coming to maturity. For the Jews this happened at age thirty. The boy Jesus, who confounded the wise among the priests and scribes at the temple, had to humble himself and go home with Joseph and Mary. He had to wait another eighteen years even though he already knew who his real Father was (Luke 2:49-52).

Jesus Christ is the one who is perfect and mature. We can never attain this on our own. Yet if we trust him, his life and his words can flow forth even from little children. The journey from Egypt to the Promised Land could have been accomplished in as little as eleven days, but all those who were disobedient and filled with unbelief spent forty years dying in the wilderness, going around and around the same mountain (Deuteronomy 1:2-3).

Notice that when the fullness of the Spirit came upon Jesus

at the Jordan River, it did not lead him to grandstand or do things that would attract attention to himself.

> 12 *And immediately the Spirit drove him into the wilderness.*

> 13 *And he was there in the wilderness forty days and forty nights and was tempted of Satan and was with the wild beasts, and the angels ministered unto him.*

When Jesus came into the fullness of the inheritance from his real Father and of the Holy Spirit, the first things that happened were some tremendous trials.

When we receive new things, when new avenues open up, when we receive new gifts, when we come into money or other forms of prosperity, new temptations will always be there.

What will we do with all of this?

Some people have done well with the Lord while they were in prison or in a concentration camp in another country. Then, after many years, they were able to escape or were released and found their way to North America, where they subsequently went down the drain in the land of plenty and prosperity.

Why?

When the rain (of blessing) falls, it waters all the seeds in the garden. When fertilizer is applied, it fertilizes everything growing in the field. If thorns and briers are in our hearts, prosperity will cause them to prosper also. Everything will come up together.

For this reason, the Lord starts us out in a desert (spiritual or otherwise). He wants to make sure no weeds are left in our hearts. Each time we receive something new and excellent from God, it will be accompanied by a test. We have not just received a new gift or talent or capacity from God; we have also received a test on how we will use it. We can use it according to the will of God for the kingdom of God and the good of others, or we can use it for personal gain and foment our own pride and arrogance.

I know of many sad stories here in Colombia of those who cultivated drugs and got involved in the drug trade, thinking about all the good they would do with the money. Instead, they were destroyed by their own avarice.

14 Now after John was put in prison, Jesus came into Galilee, preaching the gospel of the kingdom of God

John was put in prison for preaching the truth to King Herod. Later, they chopped off his head. When John was beheaded, Jesus sent forth his disciples with authority and power. After that, they were called apostles. No religious commissioning service is recorded (Mark 6:7-30). The typology is interesting. According to Scripture, there was none born of women greater than John the Baptist, yet the least in the kingdom of God is greater than he (Matthew 11:11).

What did Jesus mean by this?

In our human condition, even with gifts and callings and ministries from God, the maximum that we can expect to attain is equality with John the Baptist. However, entering the kingdom of God puts us in a different realm. We must lose our own headship and come under Jesus Christ. John understood that he was to decrease so that Christ could increase (John 3:30).

Paul wrote that he was a prisoner of the Lord (Ephesians 4:1). The Lord desires to take us prisoner so we can no longer implement our own will. The way of the cross is the same. The cross is not an instantaneous death – no bullet to the head of the old man. The cross is a long, slow, agonizing death to the old man as he loses his lifeblood of the nature of Adam drop by drop. However, if we are nailed to the cross with Jesus, we will not be able to accomplish our own will.

14 *Jesus came into Galilee, preaching the gospel of the kingdom of God*

15 *and saying, The time is fulfilled, and the kingdom of God is at hand; repent ye and believe the gospel.*

Notice that Jesus picked up on John's message of repentance and added another step. Repent and believe! Believe the gospel. Trust and depend upon the new king. You do not have to continue under Satan's kingdom of darkness.

The time is fulfilled! Now, today, if you hear his voice and have faith in him, he will grant sufficient grace and mercy to accomplish his will. The gospel of Jesus Christ involves repentance and faith, which, even if we are willing, can only be accomplished in us by his grace (power).

16 *Now as he walked by the sea of Galilee, he saw Simon and Andrew his brother casting a net into the sea, for they were fishers.*

17 *And Jesus said unto them, Follow me, and I will make you fishers of men.*

18 *And straightway they forsook their nets and followed him.*

Jesus did not say, "Follow me and I will make you hunters of men. I will give you some sharp arrows and you will shoot men with the truth." No, he told them he would teach them to fish for men. This requires patience.

My father is a good fisherman because he has more patience than I do. He is fond of telling me that his secret is very simple. To be a good fisherman, you must be smarter than the fish! You must have what they desire, know where they are, and be prepared to give up a lot of time.

Hunting is different.

True disciples must leave everything if they are to become

fishers of men. Many would-be evangelists today are not prepared to do this. They desire to be in the ministry, but they are not willing to leave their pride and arrogance behind. They cling to their own criteria. They will not leave the doctrines of men. They continue to foment their own kingdoms. They insist on retaining their boats and nets and equipment, but the Lord does not need any of this.

> 19 *And when he had gone a little further from there, he saw James the son of Zebedee and John his brother, who also were in the ship mending their nets.*

> 20 *And straightway he called them; and leaving their father Zebedee in the ship with the hired servants, they went after him.*

> 21 *And they entered into Capernaum, and straightway on the Sabbath days he entered into the synagogue and taught.*

> 22 *And they marvelled at his learning, for he taught them as one that had power with him, and not as the scribes.*

> 23 *And there was in their synagogue a man with an unclean spirit, and he cried out,*

Jesus often ministered in *their synagogue.* He went to where they, in their religion, had added thousands of things to the Word of God. The law of Moses does not mention synagogues, yet they had them then. In this passage, we see the man with the unclean spirit in "their" synagogue, but it took a clean word from God to silence and cast out the unclean spirit.

When men foment religion, they attract unclean spirits instead of the Holy Spirit. These spirits may seem like the Holy Spirit to those who lack discernment. Notice what this spirit said (in the verse below). Is this what you think a demon might say?

*24 saying, Let us alone; what have we to do with
thee, thou Jesus of Nazareth? Art thou come to
destroy us? I know thee who thou art, the Holy One
of God.*

This demon spoke like many preachers today: "The Holy One
of God, Jesus of Nazareth, comes to destroy all the ungodly."
Have you ever heard this message preached? This message was
coming from a demon, but Jesus did not say, "Very well, he is
preparing the way for my message; he has identified me cor-
rectly; he knows who I am."

No, this is what the Lord said:

*25 And Jesus rebuked him, saying, Be silent, and
come out of him.*

*26 And the unclean spirit tore him and cried with a
loud voice and came out of him.*

*27 And they were all amazed, insomuch that they
questioned among themselves, saying, What thing
is this?*

The person with the unclean spirit may have been one of the
most eloquent doctors of the law. The clear teaching of those
synagogues was that the Messiah would come and destroy
everything with fire and impose a Golden Age for Israel. The
demon started off along this line, but this was not the line that
Jesus came to preach when he opened his mouth to announce
the gospel. He did not say he had come to destroy, but rather
to save. Destruction, however, did come as the result of them
not receiving him or his message.

Jesus did not come fulminating with condemnation. He
said, *Blessed are the poor in spirit, for theirs is the kingdom of
the heavens* (Matthew 5:3).

Jesus came to right our misconceptions. In addition to

calling us to repentance, He came to encourage, to lift us up, and to cause us to understand. The *poor in spirit* in Greek are really the "poor in pride." Jesus was asking them to allow God to deal with their pride, so he might become their king. He said this in a manner that was comprehensible to those who had been baptized by John, yet this was unintelligible to arrogant religious people.

> *22 And they marveled at his learning, for he taught them as one that had power with him, and not as the scribes.*

Notice this progression: First came the event at the Jordan River when Jesus submitted to a baptism that John did not think was necessary, but Jesus chose to identify with death from the very beginning. Then came trials and testing in the wilderness. Then a clean word came forth in their synagogue that was able to confront, silence, and cast out the religious spirit they had mistaken for God. Then miracles began to flow.

> *27 And they were all amazed, insomuch that they questioned among themselves, saying, What thing is this? What new doctrine is this? for he commands the unclean spirits with power, and they obey him.*
>
> *28 And immediately his fame spread abroad throughout all the region round about Galilee.*
>
> *29 And forthwith, when they were come out of the synagogue, they entered into the house of Simon and Andrew, with James and John.*
>
> *30 But Simon's mother-in-law lay sick of a fever, and soon they told him of her.*
>
> *31 And he came and took her by the hand and lifted*

her up; and the fever left her by and by, and she ministered unto them.

32 In the evening, when the sun was down, they brought unto him all that were diseased and those that were possessed with devils.

33 And all the city was gathered together at the door.

34 And he healed many that were sick of diverse diseases and cast out many devils and suffered not the devils to speak because they knew him.

35 And in the morning, rising up a great while before day, he went out and departed into a solitary place and prayed there.

This is backward to what many do today. They start by advertising that many miracles will occur in the great meetings at the stadium that they have rented. They sell tickets and encourage the people to prepare their offerings in exchange for blessings.

Jesus spent his first twelve years under the law of his father and mother. Then he voluntarily spent another eighteen years at home without being in the limelight. According to Scripture, he grew in grace and in favor before God and before men, until God declared his approval of him in the waters of the Jordan when he demonstrated his willingness to lay down his life. John declared that Jesus was the Lamb of God who had come to take away the sin of the world. Jesus received the fullness of the inheritance of his true Father. This is the Spirit without measure (John 3:34).

Then the Devil tempted Jesus in the wilderness. Satan showed him all the kingdoms of the world, but Jesus turned down the Devil's offer.

How did the Devil show Jesus all those kingdoms?

The Devil can also give visions. The Devil showed him all

these things and supernaturally took him to the pinnacle of the temple. He wanted to tempt Jesus to show off in front of the crowd. These were tremendous experiences (Matthew 4:1-11). Many who go through this type of testing come out saying they have received great things from God, when in reality the visions and experiences have come from the Devil, the prince of this world.

Jesus rejected all of this. He was then able to go to "their synagogue," and uncover, silence, and evict their religious spirit with a word. The unclean demon spirit had been preaching what appeared to be great things, but he did not preach the message of the Lord, the gospel of the kingdom. What the unclean religious spirit had been preaching was not good news for anyone, and Jesus put a stop to it.

Today we still have churches and synagogues full of demons preaching messages that many believe are from God, yet they are not the Word of God. The most dangerous lies are those that have the highest content of truth. Rat poison is only 1-percent poison, and the other 99 percent is rat food. If it were the other way around, no rat would be so stupid as to eat the poison.

Demons inspire people to preach what appears to be the Word of God, but a problem exists. They try to keep us centered on our own lives and on how to use God to get what we want. God wants us to leave our own life behind, so we can enter into his life. The Devil tells people that God wants to see them destroyed (unless they jump through all the hoops of religion). God wants us to leave the old behind, so we may be blessed in his life.

It is not just the message; it is not just about the truth. The way in which things are presented causes a problem. Only the Lord has the anointing that breaks the yoke. After Jesus silenced the unclean spirit in their synagogue was when the miracles began. This process gathered force, not in the synagogue but in the house of Peter and Andrew. Then, after the entire town had been blessed and enthused, Jesus got up early and disappeared!

What great, well-known preacher of today, after winning a huge battle with demon spirits, performing many miracles, and congregating the entire city, would walk away from it all and disappear in the middle of the night? Many preachers today continue to fill the stadiums; they continue to take offerings; they continue to proselytize the people; and they continue to have the people fill out "decision" cards to foment their churches and organizations as long as it is possible.

> 35 *And in the morning, rising up a great while before day, he went out and departed into a solitary place and prayed there.*

> 36 *And Simon and those that were with him followed after him.*

> 37 *And when they had found him, they said unto him, All men seek for thee.*

Lord, you don't understand. Lord, look what you just started and we have to consolidate this. We have to make sure that all those new people get inducted into the synagogue, so all the local scribes and Pharisees can "follow up."

> 38 *And he said unto them, Let us go into the next towns that I may preach there also, for truly I came forth for that purpose.*

> 39 *And he preached in their synagogues throughout all Galilee and cast out devils.*

Their synagogues were scattered throughout Galilee, and they were all full of devils! Notice that he cast the devils out of Galilee from the very start, and later, when he was definitely rejected, they could not blame the devils because he had cleaned them out. He was rejected because the people did not wish to surrender to the true King. If Jesus were to reign, it would mean the end of their lives, the end of their synagogues, and the end of their religion. Even so, Jesus continued to preach the gospel during the allotted time.

> 40 *And a leper came to him, beseeching him and kneeling down to him and saying unto him, If thou wilt, thou canst make me clean.*

> 41 *And Jesus, having mercy on him, put forth his hand and touched him and said unto him, I will; be thou clean.*

> 42 *And as soon as he had spoken, immediately the leprosy departed from him, and he was clean.*

> 43 *And he straitly charged him and forthwith sent him away*

> 44 *and said unto him, See thou say nothing to any man, but go, show thyself to the priest, and offer for thy cleansing those things which Moses commanded, for a testimony unto them.*

> 45 *But he went out and began to publish it much and to blaze abroad the matter, insomuch that Jesus could no more openly enter into the city, but was without in desert places; and they came to him from every quarter.*

Leprosy is also a symbol of terminal sin. It does not matter how bad the leprosy, how bad the sin, or how bad the problem that we are in; if the Lord gives the order for us to become clean, we will become clean. If the Lord decides to touch us in our unclean state, he does not become unclean like us; we become clean like him!

Notice that Jesus did not desire the credit. Many preachers

today do not pass this test. If a blind person or a leper or some-one who is crippled is healed under their ministry, they are not capable of instructing the person to tell no one. No, they want to start another crusade! They publicize their ministry according to the ways of the world to attract attention and manage the crowd.

Jesus did not come to attract attention to himself, and he is the model for all of us. He came to glorify his Father in heaven.

Nevertheless, the former leper was unable to keep his mouth shut, and Jesus became even more famous. Note that this all happens in the first chapter of the gospel.

Why did Jesus no longer openly enter the city?

Because he was announcing and seeking a kingdom that is not of this world. He later told Pilate that if his kingdom had been of this world, his followers would have fought for it (with earthly weapons). He also told Pilate that all those who love and seek the truth are really seeking him. Pilate did not even know what the truth was. Pilate asked, *What is truth?* And the Truth was standing in person right in front of him (John 18:36-38).

The anointing that destroys the yokes of sin, leprosy, sick-ness, demons, and *their synagogues* only comes with the person of Jesus Christ, but he has other criteria for his kingdom. His kingdom is different. His kingdom is not of this world. His true ministers do not seek their own glory. This is the witness of Simon Peter.

Let us pray:

Lord, we ask that we may be able to see with greater clarity. We desire that your life and your kingdom may be seen in us, that there may be a great company of those like Elijah, like John the Baptist, to prepare the way for what you are planning to do next. May we do your will, under your headship, under your author-ity. May we receive your covering and feed exclusively on your word. Amen.

CHAPTER 2

Sent by God

Peter wrote two letters near the end of his life of service to the Lord. The thoughts in these letters were very important to him and obviously they were very important to God. Given by inspiration of the Holy Spirit and preserved in the Scriptures, the books of 1 and 2 Peter are available for us today.

1 Peter 1

1 Peter, apostle of Jesus, the Christ, to the strangers scattered in Pontus, in Galatia, in Cappadocia, in Asia, and in Bithynia,

What or who is an apostle? Today, many people talk about missionaries, but not much is said about present-day apostles. Others employ the term *apostle* when referring to being at the top of a pyramid hierarchy.

A missionary is a person sent to propagate the gospel, but sometimes we do not know who sent the missionary. God could send a missionary, or a given congregation could send them, or some denomination could send them.

Many missionaries have been sent forth on human terms, because a sending group with resources decided to send a missionary. Some groups who decided to train missionaries and send them forth did so because they desired to propagate the same religious expression that they had.

In many missionary matters, the things of God can get

mixed in with the things of men, or the things of men can take first place.

In the New Testament use of the word, an *apostle* is someone sent by God with the purpose of building up the church (and if we are part of the body of Christ, we are the church). This is very different from the person who has only been sent out by some human group or who thinks they are in charge of a group or movement.

If we study the case of Paul, who had been Saul of Tarsus and was sent as an apostle to the Gentiles, Scripture relates that Paul was an elder among a group of Christians in the church (or congregation) at Antioch. In this setting, *elder* means he was one of the people with the God-given responsibility to maintain due order in the meetings and set a good example for others.

This group had been ministering to the Lord and fasting when the Holy Spirit said, *Separate me Barnabas and Saul for the work unto which I have called them* (Acts 13:2).

The Scripture is clear that it was the Holy Spirit that sent them forth. God himself sent Paul on his missionary journeys.

Peter was also an apostle sent by God. The book of The Acts of the Apostles declares that Peter was an apostle sent to the Jews, and Paul was an apostle sent to the Gentiles. However, Paul still maintained a love and burden for his countrymen, the Jews. Some crossing over does exist, because when Peter wrote his letters, Jerusalem had probably already been (or was being) destroyed. Peter was writing to both Jews and Gentiles who were living in all the interesting places (far from the land of Israel); therefore, he addresses them as *strangers*.

> *2 chosen (according to the foreknowledge of God the Father) in sanctification of the Spirit, to obey and be sprinkled with the blood of Jesus, the Christ, Grace and peace, be multiplied unto you.*

This is a very interesting concept: Grace and peace can be multiplied.

We contemplate grace and peace and sometimes think they are something that a person either has or does not have; but this verse indicates that grace and peace can come in many different sizes. One may have a little grace and a little peace; or these qualities may be multiplied until they begin to flow forth from us and touch other people.

For grace and peace relate to the presence of the Lord.

The Lord applies grace when he comes and cleanses us and saves us and lifts us up to serve him; he does this to extend his peace. This happens because his peace is bound to his presence, even though at first this presents a conflict.

People who have the indwelling presence of the Lord reigning and ruling from the most intimate part of their being can be at peace regardless of external circumstances. A war might be going on around them, or they can be in the midst of a natural disaster and be at peace.

> 3 *Praised be the God and Father of our Lord Jesus,*
> *the Christ, who according to his great mercy has*
> *begotten us again unto a living hope by the resurrec-*
> *tion of Jesus, the Christ, from the dead,*

The resurrection is the key to understanding the new birth, which is the beginning of the power of the resurrection being applied to us.

We also see in this verse that the Lord Jesus has a God and Father. Therefore, the Lord Jesus cannot be the same, exact person as God the Father. This is clear in this verse. Jesus submits to his Father because his Father is God unto him, even though the Lord Jesus is also God, and both have the same divine nature.

The Father and the Son have two different personalities; they are two different persons, but the Lord Jesus decided to bow to the will of his Father. There is no conflict of wills. The will of the Lord Jesus is aligned with the will of the heavenly Father, because the Lord Jesus decided to operate in this manner.

One of the reasons he chose to do this was to give an example to us. He desires that we make the same choice and submit to his will, so there will be no conflict between our will and the will of the Lord Jesus Christ. Then he will send us the Holy Spirit (Acts 5:32). This way a union can be formed between the Lord Jesus and us, like the union between Jesus and his Father. This allows us to participate in the divine nature (2 Peter 1:4) by the Holy Spirit.

We will see the evidence of this in greater detail in the second epistle of Peter, but the foundation is being laid now.

> 3 *who according to his great mercy has begotten us*
> *again unto a living hope*

Notice that hope has something to do with this.

What are we to hope for?

Hope for an inheritance and also hope for the fullness of redemption.

Just as the Lord comes to live and to reign in us, he desires us to experience the fullness of his resurrection life. He desires to bring us forth in resurrection, but to do this he must take us to the cross to be crucified with him and to rid us of our evil desires and everything that is not useful to God. All that is not approved by God must be destroyed. Any possibility or inclination we might have to create our own kingdom or attempt to be God, or impose our will over the will of God, must be nipped in the bud and dealt with. Even what we think is good must be placed upon the altar of God.

This will enable us to attain:

> 4 *unto the incorruptible inheritance that cannot be*

defiled and that does not fade away, conserved in
the heavens for you,

The heavenly realms are where we can perceive the reality of God as he is. This is the spiritual realm and God is spirit. We must worship him in spirit and in truth. When we are here in flesh and blood upon this earth, we can only perceive God through the Spirit. Unless we are born again by the Holy Spirit, we do not have the faculty to perceive God. Unless we are born again, we are only able to perceive God indirectly. For example:

If the Spirit of God is governing a human being, we will be able to see the quality, the love, the graciousness, and the faith in action. Through this, we have a second-hand reflection of how God is working in and through that individual. But we will have no direct perception of God unless we have been born again by the Spirit.

Being born again by the Spirit is similar to being born the first time by flesh and blood. We were born and then we began living in a new dimension, perceiving light. Little by little our senses started to function.

All of the senses of the baby function differently after birth. Prior to birth, a baby cannot perceive light because all is dark in the womb. After birth, the light is a great stimulus that causes an indelible impression upon the newborn. The same thing happens when the person, born again by the Spirit, enters into the realm of the light of God. This leaves them shaken with an indelible impression. Little by little the senses all begin to function, vision clears up, hearing is fine-tuned, taste is diversified, and so on.

The Lord's desire is to develop all of our spiritual senses so we might love, we might perceive the glory of God, and we might have spiritual discernment.

The inheritance we are to receive cannot fade or be contaminated.

5 *who are kept in the virtue of God by faith,*

Here we can begin to understand why some Scriptures say that we must keep ourselves, and why others say that God keeps us.

The explanation for this lies in the fact that the virtue is of God and the power is of God, but we must remain firm in our faith in the Lord. This faith is not only faith in the Lord, not only believing *in* the Lord, but also believing the Lord. This is the trial of our faith (1 Peter 1:7). We must believe what he says to us when he calls us to holiness, in order to believe that he is really calling us to holiness; he is really calling us to be separated exclusively to himself from the desires and cares of the things of this world.

If we seek first the kingdom of God and his righteousness, then all the things we need from the world around us will be provided without us having to worry about them.

On the other hand, we should seek the true riches that will never fade or be corrupted and are part of our inheritance in Christ, reserved in the heavens for us.

5 *who are kept in the virtue of God by faith, to attain unto the saving health which is made ready to be manifested in the last time.*

Saving health?

The Hebrew and Greek each have two different words which were all translated as *salvation* in most English Bibles. In old Spanish, one of these words was translated *health*, and the other word was translated *salvation*, based on the work of early reformers, such as the rendition of Psalm 67:2, which still remains in the King James Bible. These two words are separated in the Jubilee Bible.

The *last time* mentioned here is the day of the Lord, which is the time that is immediately upon our prophetic horizon.

> 6 *In which ye greatly rejoice, though now for a season, if need be, ye are afflicted in diverse temptations,*

Here is a lot of truth in a very small amount of space. First, if need be, there will be afflictions and diverse temptations.

Therefore, we should rejoice if this is happening to us. It means we have been recognized as sons of our Father in heaven, and the Lord is allowing us to pass through tests and afflictions to refine us.

The verse says: *if need be.*

God may deem it necessary for us to pass through afflictions even as his sons. If it were not necessary, he would not allow this to come upon us. He only allows the afflictions and temptations that are necessary.

Some brethren do not understand what God is doing; therefore, they fail the test. After a few months or years, the Lord allows them to pass through the same test, and they fail again.

They cannot understand that if they overcome the temptation in the power of God, they will not be required to go around the same mountain over and over again. Some are facing the same test for the second, third, or maybe even for the tenth time.

These tests indicate whether we are seeking the kingdom of God and his righteousness above all else, or if we are seeking personal benefit. Much of the time, those who are being tested are not even aware that this is what is happening.

> 7 *that the trial of your faith, being much more precious than of gold (which perishes, nevertheless it is tried with fire), might be found unto praise and glory and honour when Jesus, the Christ, is made manifest;*

Jesus, the Christ, will be revealed from heaven just as he ascended. But before this, he may be made manifest in us because he desires to reign from the most intimate place in us – our hearts. But he will only be revealed in us if our hearts are clean.

Many received the earnest or down payment of the Spirit when they entered into a covenant with God. This has come with certain gifts and talents from God. However, to receive the fullness of the inheritance, our hearts must be pure and clean. Without pureness of heart, God will not release the fullness of the inheritance.

When he releases the fullness of the inheritance, a manifestation of the Lord Jesus Christ will appear in and through us of much greater magnitude than anything we have seen or experienced before.

> 8 *whom having not seen, ye love; in whom, though*
> *at present ye see him not, yet believing, ye rejoice*
> *with joy unspeakable and full of glory;*
>
> 9 *receiving the end of your faith, even the saving*
> *health of your souls.*

The end of our faith is that God will bring health and salvation to our soul. The soul is our being. It contains our personality, our will, our emotions, and everything that distinguishes us from other people.

In the New Testament, a separation exists between body, soul, and spirit; but in the Old Testament, no such division is evident. The soul is the essence or life of the person in its totality in the Old Testament.

And what does the Lord desire to do with us?

His plan is greater than just saving us from our corrupt, degenerate, unclean state. He desires a salvation that is healthy. He desires to bring us into good health (spiritually and naturally), which is his life flowing in and through us (Romans 5:10). He desires the scars in our souls, our personalities, and our emotions that may have been affected by our rebellion to be healed. He desires to cut the control of the flesh and crucify our carnal lusts. All of this must die, but he desires to restore our soul.

David said, *He restores my soul* (Psalm 23).

How will he do this?

He will regenerate us into the image and likeness of God because that was the condition of the human race at the beginning. He plans to renew us above and beyond his original design.

In what sense will we be restored back into the image and likeness of God?

The nature of God will be flowing in us because the life of Jesus Christ will be flowing in us. And the life of God is eternal life. The Lord Jesus is the life, and if we have him, we will know that we have eternal life. If we do not have him, we do not have anything (John 5:26; 1 John 5:10-13).

> 9 *receiving the end of your faith, even the saving health of your souls.*

> 10 *Of which saving health the prophets, (who prophesied of the grace that was to come in you) have enquired and searched diligently;*

In the time of the prophets of the Old Testament, the possibility did not exist of being born again and having the Holy Spirit resident in all of God's people. Only with the coming of the Lord Jesus Christ, with his death and resurrection, with his victory over death and his ascension to the right hand of the Father with all power and authority, was he able to send his Spirit. He now mediates the New Covenant from a position of complete power and authority.

The prophets inquired diligently,

> 11 *searching when and in what point of time the Spirit of Christ which was in them did signify, which*

announced beforehand the afflictions that were to
come upon the Christ, and the glory that should fol-
low them.

12 Unto whom it was revealed that not unto them-
selves, but unto us they did administer the things,
which are now announced unto you by those that
have preached the gospel unto you by the Holy Spirit
sent down from heaven, which things the angels
desire to look into.

God is doing things that we still do not understand well. A rebellion has been taking place in heaven between some of the angels and the Lord (Revelation 12:7-9). God has been using the church to teach certain things to the angels that remained faithful. Most of the time we do not understand the magnitude of what God is doing. We do not understand why the Lord is so strict regarding details that do not seem to be a big deal to us, but he needs to have a clean people.

Therefore, he is working, he is testing, and he is demonstrating certain things to the entire universe. Some day we will understand more about what is happening. I am completely convinced that when we are fighting against some temptation, some test where we have failed several times and the Lord wants to bring us through it victorious in him, this struggle is not just for our own benefit.

The person who wins one of these battles does not just win the battle; he or she also wins the possibility of helping other people who are passing through the same type of situation.

When we pass the test and overcome the temptation by the grace of God, the victory does not just affect us. This victory has eternal implications with the possibility of influencing others. It might even become part of the lesson that God is showing the angels.

> 13 *Therefore, having the loins of your understanding*
> *girded with temperance, wait perfectly in the grace*
> *that is presented unto you when Jesus, the Christ, is*
> *manifested unto you,*

First, I want to emphasize the word *temperance*. This is a word that has been taken out of and replaced in many Bibles.

Centuries ago, the old teachers of the Word said there were cardinal virtues and one of them was temperance.

What is temperance?

Temperance is doing everything in the proper measure without excess or being overcome or obsessed when the Spirit of God is governing our life. Temperance is when our appetites are under his control and under his timing, for this keeps us from going to extremes.

Temperance is being led by the Spirit of God, for where the Spirit of the Lord is, there is liberty, and we will be able to enjoy this liberty without going overboard. The person without temperance will never be satisfied no matter what they are able to obtain and no matter what they decide to prohibit (religious people tend to prohibit whatever they cannot control). They will oscillate between the two extremes of austerity and opulence, of legalism and licentiousness.

> 13 *Therefore, having the loins of your understanding*
> *girded with temperance,*

It is important to note that temperance begins with the *loins of your understanding.*

What does Peter mean by *loins*?

This word refers to our reproductive organs that must be girded (clothed) so we will not be ashamed in public.

What does *having the loins of your understanding girded with temperance* mean?

When we understand truth from God, the first thing that

occurs to many of us is to immediately apply (or reproduce) what we have learned (or what we think we have learned) to others before we have properly assimilated and digested it ourselves.

People who are living in temperance (which is a fruit of the Spirit) will receive a measure of truth and digest it and apply it quietly under the guidance (or covering) of the Spirit. They will wait until they are a victorious example before attempting to teach others (and this they will do with great caution and only as they are led step by step by the Spirit of God).

Those without temperance will always be at one extreme or the other. When they start to see the other side of the coin, they immediately go to the opposite extreme and attempt to straighten everyone else out. They always want to take the speck out of the eye of their brother or sister while the beam is still in their own eye (Matthew 7:3).

Those who do not have the loins of their understanding girded with temperance will continue to present a spectacle just as bad as when someone runs around naked or improperly clothed in public.

Remember King Uzziah? He was not born into the priesthood, but he foolishly insisted on entering the Holy Place of the temple. Then he was smitten with leprosy (2 Chronicles 26:16-21).

Remember what happened with his son Jotham (2 Chronicles 27:2)? Scripture relates that he was a just king, but he would not go into the temple because his father had contracted leprosy in the temple.

Why did his father come down with leprosy?

It was because King Uzziah insisted on entering the inner court of the temple that was exclusively reserved for the priests. Only those who had been born into the priesthood of the sons of Aaron were allowed to enter the Holy Place of the temple. The king, however, had legal responsibilities before God and before the people that required his presence in the outer court of the temple next to the pillar, but now the son of Uzziah refused to do this.

Why?

Because since the father exceeded his liberty by going too far inside the temple, the son exceeded the restriction by never going back even to the outer court of the temple.

This is typical human behavior.

If we continue to operate in the realm of the grass that withers or the flower that fades, and if we never enter into the Word of the Lord that endures forever, we will continue to vacillate from one extreme to another.

We all know of friends who have gone to extremes regarding the things of God. If we honestly examine our hearts, we would all have to admit that at one time or another we have gone to extremes as well.

Temperance is a virtue of God; it is a fruit of the Spirit. God desires to find this good fruit in his people as his nature begins to come to maturity in us. The Lord Jesus was showing forth temperance when he went and ate and drank at the houses of the publicans and sinners, yet remained without sin.

Temperance is a sign of maturity, and those who desire to come to maturity in Christ will take heed:

> *13 Therefore, having the loins of your understanding girded with temperance, wait perfectly in the grace that is presented unto you when Jesus, the Christ, is manifested unto you,*

> *14 as obedient sons, not conforming yourselves with the former desires that you had before in your ignorance,*

We are to handle the revelation and grace that we receive from the Lord with temperance. The Lord walked in temperance, and if we walk by his side in yoke with him, we will also walk in temperance in all that we say or do as he continues to effect a total cleansing of our hearts.

> 15 *but as he who has called you is holy, so be ye holy in all manner of conversation;*

> 16 *for it is written, Be ye holy; for I am holy.*

Here the word *conversation* means "behavior." It is our talk and our walk.

What does it mean to be holy?

Being holy is to be separated from the things and appetites and desires of this world unto the Lord, so we may flow and work according to the nature of God. Until we enter into the nature of God, we cannot know true satisfaction. We cannot be satisfied unless we hunger and thirst for righteousness (Matthew 5:6).

> 17 *And if ye invoke as Father, he who without respect for persons judges according to the work of each one, converse in fear the entire time of your sojourning here,*

This means that we are on a pilgrimage in the sense that while we live here, the Lord will take us from one place to another. He directs us on the path to become the mature sons of God who will receive and manage the inheritance. He can only accomplish this if he has been able to cleanse our hearts.

Therefore, he desires to free us from our fears of things and authorities or powers or rulers of this world so we are motivated only by the authentic fear of God the Father.

Fear of God the Father?

This is not a terrorist type of fear; it is a fear of respect. It is a profound fear of not offending God in anything that we are saying or doing. He desires for us to live like this.

> 18 *knowing that ye have been ransomed from your vain*

*conversation (which you received from your fathers),
not with corruptible things like silver and gold,*

*19 but with the precious blood of the Christ, as of a
lamb without blemish and without contamination,*

We had been slaves of our own desires, possessing a fallen
nature that we received through Adam and our natural fathers,
but now we have been ransomed with the blood of Christ and
born again into the nature of God the Father.

Therefore, we must now learn to manage the true riches.
When we are born again, we receive the earnest or down payment of our inheritance. We have the gifts of the Spirit to see
if we will be faithful with a little, if we will seek personal gain
in the flesh, or if we will instead seek the good of the kingdom
of God. We have been ransomed.

*19 but with the precious blood of the Christ, as of a
lamb without blemish and without contamination,*

*20 already ordained from before the foundation of
the world, but was manifest in these last times for
love of you,*

*21 who by him do believe God, who raised him up
from the dead and has given him glory: that your
faith and hope might be in God.*

*22 Having purified your souls in the obedience of the
truth, by the Spirit, in unfeigned brotherly love, love
one another with a pure heart fervently,*

This is beyond believing in God. We are to believe God and
do what he says.

Therefore, we must place our faith in God, which will lead
us to obedience as he tells us to *love one another with a pure
heart fervently.*

Obedience to what?

Obedience to the truth by the Spirit. And as we take these steps of obedience to the Lord, we will notice that this is not done by the flesh but by the Spirit; this is done by the work of God in us and will result in a pure heart so God can then work through us.

A pure heart is not the result of our own works; it does not come by joining a convent or interning in a place where someone else tells us what to do. It does not come by keeping rules or attending meetings or masses. It does not come by memorizing verses. It does not come by reciting litanies of "Our Father" or attempting to practice the Ten Commandments or any such thing.

It comes by obeying the truth by the Holy Spirit until our conscience is clean.

22 *Having purified your souls in the obedience of the truth, by the Spirit,*

The truth is a person. The Lord Jesus is the truth. It is important that we understand this process of sanctification – how we can come to have a pure heart.

Many times I have felt that the Lord told me something, and then I said to myself, *Was that really God?* Why did I question if it was really the Lord speaking to me? Because if I had done what the Lord had asked, my flesh and my pride and my arrogance would have been humbled.

The other option was to not do what the Lord was saying to me. If I didn't do it, something else would have happened: The Lord would have begun to lift his peace. Sometimes he does not lift it completely, but the peace of the Lord begins to withdraw and the intimate communion with him becomes more and more distant. If we make a mistake and decide to not obey his voice, he will not instantly cut us off, but the Holy

Spirit will be grieved. If our heart is joined to his heart, we will be grieved also.

If we have ever had the peace that passes understanding, we will know when that peace is shaken or removed. After years of being led and guided by his peace, I know when it begins to be affected. I know, at that point, that the Lord has something he wants to show me.

Sometimes he wants me to pray and intercede for someone else. But other times when I did something I should not have done or failed to do something I should have done, the Lord might desire immediate correction. If I stop everything and go and do what the Lord is asking, the full restoration of his peace will return.

22 *love one another with a pure heart fervently,*

23 *being born again, not by corruptible seed, but of incorruptible, by the word of God, which lives and abides for ever.*

The corruptible seed is the word invented by men. This occurs when men preach the things of God on their own (or with the help of spirits that are not holy). The incorruptible seed is when God gives the authority. He sends the preacher and the message flows from his heart, a pure heart. This seed is incorruptible.

When this seed is planted in someone's heart and the person embraces this word, the seed will germinate and grow: First the blade, then the flower, and finally the fullness of the fruit of the Holy Spirit (Mark 4:28). This is the process that the Lord has for each and every one of us.

This is much more than repeating a "sinner's prayer." It requires inviting the living Word to speak to us, give us direction, and order our lives. He will uncover all iniquity (hidden sin we hold to) and eradicate all our rebellion (doing the opposite of what God wants). He will correct situations, ask for the impossible, and straighten out embarrassing situations. He will restore what has been lost and win the victory in every area of sin and defeat.

Peter then quotes the prophecy of Isaiah:

24 *For all flesh is as grass, and all the glory of man as the flower of grass. The grass withers, and its flower falls away,*

25 *but the word of the Lord endures for ever. And this is the word which by the gospel is preached unto you.*

Peter, under the inspiration of the Holy Spirit, added a line to Isaiah:

25 *And this is the word which by the gospel is preached unto you.*

This is not the gospel of the blade or of the leaf; it is not the gospel of the flower; this is the gospel of the fruit that endures forever with a changed life, leaving the nature of Adam behind and entering into the nature of our Lord Jesus.

Without the fruit, someone who is immature in Christ, remaining in the stage of the blade or the flower, cannot plant this gospel of the kingdom of God. They do not have the fruit which contains the seed and, therefore, they cannot plant the gospel.

Jesus said that we will know them by their fruits (Matthew 7:16, 20). Every fruitful plant is the same. The seed is not in the leaf; it is not in the flower; it is in the fruit.

This chapter ends with this reference from Isaiah 40: All flesh is as grass, and all the glory of man as the flowers of the field. The grass withers and the flower fades, but the word of our God shall stand forever.

So, what does the Lord desire to do in us? He desires to bring us into a new birth by the Spirit.

How will he initiate this new birth? By planting a seed in each of us.

What is this seed? This seed is the Word of God. It begins with a spoken or even a written word. But in a greater context, it is the life of the Lord Jesus that will be planted in our hearts.

If the seed finds good soil in our hearts, it will grow and develop. Jesus will have control and dominate our being by the Spirit of God. He will cut everything that links us with desires that do not line up with the will of God. When our hearts are clean, the image of God will be reflected in us because our hearts are designed to mirror and reflect the glory of God. Then we will have communion not only with Jesus but also with his Father by the Holy Spirit.

The grass withers, and all flesh is grass.

This flesh is the physical tabernacle in which we are now living. It will wither sooner or later, and all of the glory of man, even everything that man can accomplish after being born again with all the gifts and talents that God gives him, will fade sooner or later.

Paul describes this in 1 Corinthians 13. This chapter centers on the love of God, which is translated as *charity* in the Reformation Bible.

1 Corinthians 13

8 *Charity is never lost, but prophecies shall come to an end, tongues shall cease, and knowledge shall come to an end.*

9 *For we know in part, and we prophesy in part.*

10 *But when that which is perfect is come, then that which is in part shall be done away.*

In the end, three things will remain:

> 13 *And now abide faith, hope, charity, these three;*
> *but the greatest of these is charity.*

Charity is the love of God.

Faith could have also been translated *faithfulness*. This is like a page written on both sides – one side is our faith, our faithfulness to the Lord; the other side is the faith of the Lord Jesus and his faithfulness to his Father.

Even if we are unfaithful, the Lord Jesus remains faithful. Therefore, if we are under his government and begin to err, he will correct us with the goal of getting us out of trouble. If we continue to receive his correction, he will bring us back on track.

How will he accomplish this? He will use fire and bitter, difficult experiences that will remove the evil desires from our hearts.

Therefore, the Lord will not cast us off if we err, unless we reject his correction. Those who repeatedly reject his correction may lose their close fellowship with the Lord. Then the Lord may stop attempting to correct them. Those who are not under the discipline and correction of the Lord are not secure, because in our relationship with him, he is our security (Matthew 7).

Why is he so interested in cleansing us from all iniquity? Because we are candidates for receiving an incorruptible inheritance that cannot be defiled and that does not fade away, reserved in the heavens for us.

Let us pray:

Heavenly Father:
We ask that we might become fruitful and display the fruit of your nature before the world, that we may be bread for the hungry and seed for the sower as we plant your nature into receptive hearts. We ask that this gospel of the kingdom may go forth and produce

a great harvest in abundance. We ask that after we have spent so much time (like the disciples) fishing all night without catching anything (or catching very little), we will become willing as individuals and as the church to hear your voice, to do your will, and to wait upon your word to cast the net to the other side, that we might see and experience the results of doing everything according to your ways and under your direct orders.

May our lives be transformed so we might become productive in your kingdom. We ask this in the name of our Lord Jesus Christ. Amen.

CHAPTER 3

Becoming a Living Stone

1 Peter 2

1 Having therefore left all malice and all guile and hypocrisies and envies and all murmurings,

2 as newborn babes, desire the rational milk of the word, that ye may grow thereby in health;

For this process to develop, the planted seed must be an incorruptible seed and not a corruptible seed that will not bear good fruit. This is the difference between the wheat and the tares.

People who enter into this new life in Christ must receive the seed, which is the Lord, and yield their life to the government of God. They must be totally repentant of having done things their own way, which requires the grace of God.

The person who is born again into the kingdom of God is like a little newborn baby who needs to be nourished with spiritual milk. This is a clean but simple word that the Lord will apply in a practical manner. As time passes, the Lord will apply stronger truth. In the realm of spiritual food, we see three stages: milk, bread, and strong food.

Scripture says that strong food belongs to those who are mature or perfect (Hebrews 5:12-14).

Peter states that the entrance requirement in order to feed on the basic milk of the Word is to have left *all malice and all guile and hypocrisies and envies and all murmurings.* The only way this can happen is if the Spirit of God is at work in our hearts.

Most of those who name the name of the Lord in Christendom today have not left these things. They have been given another list of things to leave that includes things like cigarettes, alcohol, dancing, and bad language. Then they are told to come to meetings, pay tithes and offerings, etc. A person may attempt to meet all the requirements of man and yet still be operating in the flesh. However, it is not possible to leave *all malice and all guile and hypocrisies and envies and all murmurings* while operating as a hypocrite in the flesh.

In the case of many who smoke cigarettes, for example, if God does not remove this desire from the heart, total victory is not possible. So what good does it do a person if he or she splashes on cologne and washes out their mouth with Listerine so they can fake being faithful and virtuous while attending the meeting? Nothing is gained from doing this.

In fact, a person would benefit more by arriving at the church service smelling like cigarettes, admitting the problem, and asking God to cleanse him. At the end of the day, smoking cigarettes is one of the least of the problems facing newborn Christians.

The real problems become aggravated when people make a huge self-effort and stop smoking, stop drinking, improve their vocabulary, and clean up their outward appearance but continue to be full of *all malice and all guile and hypocrisies and envies and all murmurings.* They have not allowed the Spirit of God to bring them to a full repentance, and the power of the grace of God is not yet active in their hearts.

The Lord gave many examples of this, such as the Pharisee who came and prayed, exclaiming that he was glad he was not like the poor sinner over there, while of the publican, it says that he simply *smote upon his breast, saying, God, reconcile me, a sinner* (Luke 18:9-14).

God rejected the Pharisee and justified the "sinner" publican.

> 1 *Having therefore left all malice and all guile and hypocrisies and envies and all murmurings,*

> 2 *as newborn babes, desire the rational milk of the word, that ye may grow thereby in health;*

Jesus did not come to save us *in* our sin but to save us *from* our sin. He came not only to offer us forgiveness but also to cleanse us from all iniquity and restore us to good health (Titus 2:14). The Lord begins this process of cleansing and restoration from the inside out, whereas the religion of men always wants to deal with the outside appearance first. When the heart has been cleansed and restored by the nature of God, the appetites will also be clean (Matthew 5:6). The person will no longer desire to wallow in vice and in filth. The person's vocabulary will line up with the heart of God, and he will not need to invent or copy a religious vocabulary.

Someone came up to me after a meeting one time and said, "You are in error because you are not telling the people what sins to avoid and what their religious obligations are."

I replied, "Look Brother, when you plant a fruit tree and the tree begins to grow, you will water it and apply fertilizer. After a few years, the time comes when the tree will give its first fruit. If it is an apple tree, would it be necessary to bring it a nice, big, red, juicy apple and tell the tree, 'Look, this is how your apples must be; Notice the size, notice the color, notice the texture, and be very careful to make all your apples exactly like this'? And if you do not do this, will the apples fail to turn out nice?"

"Of course not!" he replied.

Why not?

Because the quality of the fruit is manifest according to the nature of the seed and the health of the tree.

If we deal with the issues of the heart, we have only two possible seeds: one that is corruptible and one that is incorruptible.

If we embrace the incorruptible seed and allow the Lord to pull all of the weeds out of our hearts as we feed on what he says, we will produce the good fruit.

> *3 if so be ye have tasted that the Lord is benevolent;*

> *4 coming unto whom (is the living Stone, disallowed indeed of men, but chosen of God, and precious),*

> *5 ye also, as living stones, are built up a spiritual house, a holy priesthood, to offer up spiritual sacrifices, well pleasing to God by Jesus, the Christ.*

Peter was likely writing this very close to the time when the temple at Jerusalem was destroyed (or while it was being destroyed), for the Lord had said that not one stone would be left on top of another (and this is exactly what happened).

The stones of the temple had been joined by a unique construction. They were perforated with holes that passed through each stone and into the next, and the courses of stone were joined by molten gold, which had been poured down the holes. This led to the practice of the swearing of oaths by the gold of the temple (Matthew 23:16-17), while ignoring the real meaning of the temple.

What an extraordinary symbol of us as living stones joined together by the very nature of God. The Jews, however, did not understand this. The Romans who destroyed Jerusalem did understand that the gold was there, so they threw down all the stones in their search for the precious metal. The Lord, of course, knew this would happen and prophesied that not one stone would be left upon another.

Therefore, we do not need to be inventing plans about how we are going to organize the church or define ministry. We do not have to worry about who will fill a given post or who will be elders, deacons, and pastors. The Lord not only knows what he intends to do but will also show us everything we need to know if our hearts are right before him.

For quite some time now, men have been doing things according to their pleasure. The Lord has allowed this and sometimes has even blessed their efforts. However, the Lord says that the glory of this latter house will be greater than that of the former house (Haggai 2:9).

The former house was a temple built with hands by men, and the latter house is built by God with living stones. The Lord began this work at Pentecost when he sent the fire of God. But many in the church have continued to build their own versions of the "former house."

In the course of history, when Israel strayed from the will of God, they eventually (for one reason or another) allowed the fire of God to be extinguished from the altar and the lampstand. Even though this happened, no provision had been made to light another fire, but they did it anyway. In order for the glory of God to be present, the true fire of God had to be continually maintained and not some strange fire kindled by man (Leviticus 10:1-2). Two or three times God relit the fire upon the altar after times of great apostasy – once during the time of King David and once when Elijah called down fire from heaven.

However, when the tongues of fire came and relit the fire of God on the day of Pentecost, the fire was lit upon the people who were there, because now the real temple is not made of stones and gold in Jerusalem. The real temple is the body of Christ with many members built of living stones joined together by the fire and the presence of the Holy Spirit (Acts 2).

Jesus said, "Destroy this temple and I will raise it up in three days" (John 2:19; Mark 14:58).

He was explaining that he would be resurrected from the dead on the third day, but he was also speaking prophetically of a much larger picture in which one day is as a thousand years and a thousand years are as a day. During two prophetic days (two thousand years), men would continue to do things in God's name according to their own ways, but on the third day (in the third millennium at his second coming), a temple will be raised up of living stones according to his specifications.

> 6 *Therefore, also as it is contained in the scripture,*
> *Behold, I lay in Sion the chief corner stone, chosen,*
> *precious; and he that believes on him shall not be*
> *confounded.*

To believe on him is to depend on him completely.

When he comes to dwell in our hearts, to put his roots down in our hearts, he will eventually produce the fruit of righteousness in our lives if we allow him to remain in us and we remain in him (John 15:1-8).

> 7 *Unto you, therefore, who believe he is precious;*
> *but unto those who are disobedient, the stone which*
> *the builders disallowed, the same is made the head*
> *of the corner,*

> 8 *and a stone of stumbling and a rock of offense,*
> *even to those who stumble at the word, not obeying*
> *in that for which they were ordained.*

At the time that Peter was writing this, terrible things had been happening regarding the Jews in Jerusalem. Some had received and acclaimed a false messiah named Simon Bar Jesus, and others were following another candidate. According to Josephus, a great scandal and a bloody fight took place between factions of Jews that encompassed the temple mount in which the grain reserves (stored in and under the temple) were burned up and destroyed. These reserves would have sustained them for many years during the Roman siege that came upon them as a result of their rebellion.

One of the main reasons that they defied the Romans was because they were trusting in their false messiah. Jesus warned them about this:

Mark 13

14 But when ye shall see the abomination of desolation (spoken of by Daniel the prophet) standing where it ought not, he that reads, let him understand, then let those that are in Judaea flee to the mountains;

The messiah was to be both priest and king. When the Christians saw the false messiah in the Holy Place, they fled to the mountains and were saved. Everyone else was destroyed in the siege of Jerusalem by AD 70.

Jesus also said:

Luke 21

20 And when ye shall see Jerusalem compassed with armies, then know that the desolation thereof is near.

21 Then let those who are in Judaea flee to the mountains, and let those who are in the midst of it depart out, and let not those that are in the country enter thereinto.

22 For these are days of vengeance, that all things which are written may be fulfilled.

Those who had heard the Lord pronounce these words and were in communion with the Holy Spirit saw all of this happen. They had two testimonies. Simon Bar Jesus, the false messiah, was in the temple – the abomination standing where it ought not. Then the Roman armies marched on Jerusalem and for a few hours pulled back. The Christians had just enough time to flee. (Peter may have been among them.)

No one else survived. After a three-and-a-half-year siege, the Romans razed the city and completely destroyed the temple. This is all a symbol in type and shadow of what will happen at the end of the Christian era. The abomination of desolation is still active in the temple, but this time the Holy Place is a description of the church. Rebuilding the temple in Jerusalem is not necessary, even though many are attempting to do so. It is possible that they may succeed.

We, however, are the temple now, and the Holy Place is the interior part of our being that should be full of the presence of the Spirit of God. If we allow another spirit that is not holy to inhabit our Holy Place, we create an abomination of desolation because it will cause the presence of the true Holy Spirit to leave. This can occur on an individual or on a corporate level. God can withdraw his presence from entire congregations if an unclean, religious spirit is allowed to run rampant (Revelation 2:5).

Therefore, the history of the Jews in Jerusalem in AD 67 is repeating itself in Christendom at the end of the church age, and the warnings of Matthew 24, Mark 13, and Luke 21 are valid for us today.

When these things happen, we are to flee to the mountain. What mountain? The Lord is the mountain.

The lesson for today is that we must seek the direct presence and guidance of the Lord and not trust in the religious systems of men or in religious spirits that are supernatural but not holy.

There may or may not be a rebuilt temple in Jerusalem. If there is, that rebuilding will be part of a complex deception in a last desperate attempt by the Enemy to unite everyone in a vast new world religion.

The highest level of deception, however, is when the Enemy attempts to dwell in our inner being (in our holy place) by passing himself off as an angel of light. We must reject this deception, because the Enemy can do miracles and falsify spiritual gifts and experiences. The one thing that he has never been able to counterfeit, however, is the fruit of the Spirit.

Our only means of safety is to be joined directly to the Lord in the realm of the Holy of Holies. We must turn our backs upon our own desires and upon our own works. If we are willing to give up our own lives, he will live his life in and through us (Mark 8:35).

1 Peter 2

9 But ye are the chosen generation, a royal priest-hood, a holy nation, an acquired people, that ye should show forth the virtues of him who has called you out of darkness into his marvellous light.

Notice that God has acquired us (we belong to him), so we can show forth his virtues (the power of his character) as a holy nation dedicated exclusively to him. We are the chosen generation (the generation of the body of Christ), a royal priesthood. We do not belong to the order of the priesthood of Levi; we belong to the order of Melchisedec, meaning "King of Righteousness" (Hebrews 5:10; 7:1-2).

We have entered into the royal priestly family of Christ by a new birth; therefore, we may be a part of the true temple made without hands in the spiritual realm. We are now able to have direct communion by the Holy Spirit with God the Father through our Lord Jesus Christ.

The opportunity before us is much greater than any previous opportunity for those who would worship in a building made with hands. We do not need a rebuilt temple in natural Jerusalem, because we are the temple and the Lord Jesus is the chief cornerstone. We have communion with the Father and with the Son by means of the very nature of God, because we are filled with his Spirit. Therefore, we do not have to worry about what our ministry is, where we are going to serve God, how we are going to invent a strategy to further the kingdom of God, or how we are going to raise funds and recruit workers for worthy projects.

No! None of this! The Lord will place each living stone in its place. This new temple is being built without hands. Everything comes together in the nature of Christ.

> 10 *Ye who in the time past were not a people, but are now the people of God, who in the time past had not obtained mercy, but now have obtained mercy.*

Notice that Peter is clear on the fact that the gospel has now been sent to the Gentiles, and this letter is not just for Jews, but is also very inclusive of the Gentiles who have been born again. In other words, this letter is most certainly written directly for people like us.

> 11 *Dearly beloved, I beseech you as strangers and pilgrims, abstain from the carnal desires which war against the soul*

> 12 *and have your honest conversation among the Gentiles, so that, in that which they murmur about you as of evildoers, having witnessed your good works, they may glorify God in the day of visitation.*

When the systems of man are imposed upon the church, the "Gentiles" who are outside the church and do not have circumcised hearts are not able to have a good witness about what is going on in the church. They look at the "good" works devised by man, and to them, the church people appear to be evildoers.

They see every pastor as a manipulator, squeezing tithes and offerings from the people. They see every priest as a pedophile. So many bad testimonies abound that the unconverted tend to paint everyone with the same brush. Many of those who go to church and talk with pious-sounding religious language are vicious sharks and wolves when it comes to business and financial relationships.

Those who truly belong to the Lord are different from those who simply belong to organized religion. Yet we are called upon by God to respect God-ordained human authority, whether or not those in authority are converted.

> 13 *Therefore, be subject to every human ordinance*
> *that is of the Lord, whether it be to a king or to a*
> *superior,*
>
> 14 *and unto governors as unto those that are sent*
> *by him for the punishment of evildoers and for the*
> *praise of those that do well.*

Notice that this is qualified in that it says *be subject to every human ordinance that is of the Lord.*

This Scripture does not obligate us to be subject to ungodly human ordinance or authority. The very basis of all jurisprudence, the very basis for all truth, and the very basis of all justice has to have come from God. Many human governments and laws reflect this in some manner. However, men have invented many things that are not of the Lord.

When Peter refers to *every human ordinance that is of the Lord,* he is referring to the Lord Jesus Christ who is the only basis for true government. Any governor who is not ordained by him is an impostor.

> 15 *For this is the will of God, that in well doing ye may silence the ignorance of vain men,*

> 16 *as being free, yet not using your liberty to cover maliciousness, but as slaves of God.*

We are in liberty, but our liberty is not to be abused because we belong to God.

If we are operating in the liberty of the Spirit of God without maliciousness and under the direct orders of the Lord as slaves of God, we are free from the bondage of men.

As we serve God and others with a clean heart – without malice, without guile, without hypocrisy, without murmuring – do you know what will happen?

We will silence the ignorance of vain men and convince others of the goodness and greatness of God. We will convince them that we are the people of God and we are willing to give our lives for God and for our neighbor.

> 17 *Honour all men. Love the brotherhood. Fear God. Honour the king.*

The king that we are to honor above all else is Jesus Christ.

> 18 *Servants, be subject to your masters with all fear, not only to the good and humane, but also to the unjust.*

> 19 *For this is due to grace, if a man for conscience toward God endures grief, suffering wrongfully.*

> 20 *For what glory is it if, when ye are buffeted for your faults, ye shall take it patiently? but if, when ye do well and suffer for it, ye take it patiently, this is due to grace from God.*

21 *Because for this were ye called: for the Christ
also suffered for us, leaving us an example, that ye
should follow his steps*

22 *who did no sin neither was guile found in his
mouth,*

23 *who, when he was cursed, did not return the
curse; when he suffered, he did not threaten, but
committed himself to him that judges righteously;*

Friends, we are called to follow in his footsteps and overcome
evil with good in the midst of trials and tribulations. In almost
any avenue of work where we could be employed, we will have
to deal with difficult people.

If the Lord can remove from us our intense desire to defend
ourselves, the door will open for him to defend us and judge
our case as he sees fit.

This happened in the case of Stephen. He started out as
a deacon, or servant (waiting on tables so the apostles could
have more time for spiritual matters). Then God expanded his
ministry until he was performing miracles and preaching to
large crowds. In the midst of this, the enemies of the gospel
killed him (Acts 6-8).

One person behind this killing was Saul of Tarsus, and after
this, Saul went on a rampage, persecuting the church unjustly.
The Christians (including Stephen) were content to leave their
case in the hands of the Lord.

What did the Lord do?

He judged the case righteously. Jesus waited until Saul was
on the way to the city of Damascus (Scripture relates that Saul
was still breathing out threats against the Christians), and then
Jesus confronted Saul. The experience brought Saul to the ground
and left him blinded by the brightness of the glory of God. In
essence, Jesus gave Saul (later Paul) the opportunity to replace

his religious rage for the cause of Christ. Jesus told Ananias from day one that he would show Saul how much it would behoove him to suffer for the cause of Christ (Acts 9:15-16).

For the rest of his life, the apostle Paul considered himself to be the least of the apostles because he had persecuted the followers of Jesus Christ. But looking back in history, who really was Paul?

He was the apostle who helped turn the world upside down as an ambassador for Jesus. Paul was unstoppable and willing to take on any risk or hardship to fulfill the orders that he continually received from the Holy Spirit.

When he was in chains in prison, just as he had put so many others in prison, he had his most valuable ministry there. He even served the Lord in the palace of Caesar until he was martyred for his faith. Here in Colombia, more pastors have been killed over the past fifteen or twenty years than in any other country in the world. Christians have been kidnapped or put in jail on a regular basis. Even the justice system of the official government is one of the worst in the world.

When human justice fails and we leave our case in the hands of the Lord, he is always able and willing to turn things around. Some of those who attempt to kill, persecute, or imprison God's representatives may very well find themselves being drafted to replace those that they have attacked. Others may find that the very thing they attempted to do unto God's people is what, in fact, will happen to them.

Tertullian, an early church father, said that "the blood of the martyrs is the seed of the church." The gospel was extended throughout the known world, and even the seemingly invincible Roman Empire was overcome by the power of the gospel of Jesus Christ.

In our present day, in what has been prophesied as the day of the Lord, I venture to say that we have not seen anything yet. The best is yet to come. God is calling everyone to come and partake of the feast that he has prepared. When the first invited guests did not come, he repeated his invitation out into the highways and byways. He has now given orders to his servants to invite everyone, bad and good. He does not care if they are lame, blind, or maimed; the order has gone forth to compel them to come in, for:

> 24 *he himself bore our sins in his own body on the tree, that we, being dead to sins, should live unto righteousness; by whose wound ye were healed.*
>
> 25 *For ye were as sheep that had gone astray, but are now converted unto the Shepherd and Bishop of your souls.*

Note that he is the real Shepherd (pastor) and Bishop (overseer) of our souls. His work of redemption was done so we could be dead to sins and alive unto righteousness.

The greatest problem in the world today is corruption, which produces unrighteousness (injustice). This will not change until God has a people who are dead to sins and alive unto righteousness that he can put on display.

Righteousness means doing and being what God wants or desires. We can only achieve this if he is living inside of us. The governors of this world do things their way, but God does things his way. He does not force anyone. Those who receive him receive his government in their hearts; they receive a profound change in their motivation and desires. This is how the kingdom of God begins. It starts practically unobserved in the depths of the heart and soul of those who respond to the Word of God, and it grows until the fruit is of such quality and quantity that the world is unable to ignore what God has accomplished. This is the plan of God.

Let us pray:

Heavenly Father:

We ask that we might understand this message, that we might understand why this message is so different from our manner of doing things. We ask that the human plans to extend your people, to extend your church, may rapidly come to an end so we may do things your way. May we quietly yield to your government and bow before you and understand that it is your government, your kingdom that will overcome all the kingdoms of this world. Amen.

CHAPTER 4

Free to Be Slaves of Righteousness

1 Peter 3

1 *Likewise, ye wives, be in subjection to your own husbands, so that also those who do not obey the Word, may be won without a word by the conversation of their wives,*

2 *considering your chaste conversation which is in fear.*

Note that this admonition includes women with unsaved husbands.

3 *Let their adorning not be outward with ostentatious hairdos and wearing of gold nor in composition of apparel,*

4 *but let the interior adorning of the heart be without corruption, and of an agreeable spirit and peaceful, which is precious in the sight of God.*

5 *For after this manner in the old time the holy women also, who waited upon God, adorned themselves, being in subjection unto their own husbands,*

6 *as Sara obeyed Abraham, calling him lord, of whom ye are made daughters, doing well and not being afraid of any terror.*

Godly women have chaste conversation in fear of (respect

for) their husbands and the Lord, so they can do well and not be afraid of any terror. There are many problems and terrors (psychological and otherwise) that are prone to happen when divine order is not adhered to in the home.

> 7 *Likewise, ye husbands, dwell with them wisely, giving honour unto the woman, as unto a more fragile vessel and as being heirs together of the grace of life, that your prayers not be hindered.*

> 8 *And finally, be ye all of one consent, of one affection, loving each other fraternally, merciful, courteous,*

> 9 *not rendering evil for evil or curse for curse, but to the contrary, blessing, knowing that ye are called, that ye should possess a blessing by inheritance.*

Peter is speaking of flowing together in nothing less than the very nature of God. In his second letter, he follows up on this.

None of this is possible unless there has been a genuine, new spiritual birth. When we are born the first time into this world, we receive the fallen nature of our ancestor, Adam. We have a natural compulsion towards selfishness and lies. Therefore, we attempt to teach our children to be unselfish and to tell the truth. We do not need to teach a small child to lie; to the contrary, we must teach them to appreciate the truth.

Scripture states that in our natural state we are slaves to sin. We are born with this terrible compulsion due to the rebellion of our forefather, Adam. Scripture reveals that by the obedience of Jesus Christ (who is called the second Adam in Scripture), we can become slaves to righteousness and have an overwhelming inner compulsion to do what is right because a different nature, by the word of God, has been planted deep into our being. This causes the inner force of our motivation to change. The person who has been born again is not at peace if he has done something that is not right.

10 *For he that desires to love life and see the good days, let him refrain his tongue from evil and his lips that they speak no guile;*

11 *let him separate himself from evil and do good; let him seek peace and follow it.*

12 *For the eyes of the Lord are over the righteous, and his ears are open unto their prayers; but the face of the Lord is against those that do evil.*

13 *And who is he that can harm you, if ye are followers of that which is good?*

14 *But also if ye suffer anything for righteousness' sake, blessed are ye; therefore, be not afraid of their terror neither be troubled,*

15 *but sanctify the Lord God in your hearts, and be ready always to respond to every man that asks you a reason of the hope that is in you with meekness and reverence,*

We are to live in such a way that others will ask us the reason of the hope that is within us. We are to respond to their questions with meekness and reverence.

Living this kind of life is not being taught or practiced in many places today. Churches are full of spiritual fetuses who have not been born into the light, but they continue to be dedicated to multiplying the unborn.

How do they do this?

They conduct courses on evangelism and send their people out to knock on doors, pass out leaflets, or do something else to recruit proselytes. Then they indoctrinate the new recruits.

They are prone to indoctrinate people who have not had a true change of heart and who have not really been born again.

When there has truly been a new birth and the nature of God is beginning to flow through us, then things are the other way around, because God changes the person from the inside out. Then godly teaching, such as what Peter is doing in his epistles, is extremely effective. In the New Covenant, God desires to place his law in our souls and write it on our hearts (Jeremiah 31:33).

When there has been a genuine conversion, others will notice; when they notice, they will begin to ask questions; and when they ask questions, Peter admonishes us to:

> 15 *be ready always to respond to every man that*
> *asks you a reason of the hope that is in you with*
> *meekness and reverence,*

This is not like selling a commercial product. We are not to train people to evangelize as if they were closing some financial deal. We are to represent the Lord, and therefore he is the one who must send the workers (Luke 10:2). We are his ambassadors. If others notice this, then we are to always be ready to respond with meekness and reverence.

Jesus does not send us forth like traveling salesmen. Peter ought to know. The evangelism described by Peter is a far cry from what is going on in large sectors of the church. Jesus said we shall know them by their fruit (by the godly character that is being developed). Indoctrinated proselytes who only have a mental knowledge of doctrine will never produce the fruit of the Spirit. It never even dawns on them that the seed is in the fruit, and if they do not demonstrate the fruit of the Holy Spirit in their lives, they will never have any incorruptible seed to plant. It is the evidence of the delightful fruit of the Spirit in us that prompts the unsaved to ask us questions about the hope that we have.

I have found it virtually impossible to successfully evangelize someone unless (at some point) the person begins asking the right questions. If they ask us the right questions, the opportunity opens up for us to give them the right answers. Under these ideal conditions, the seed of the Word of God will be planted deep into their hearts.

This can happen at the most unexpected times. I was on an airplane traveling from Miami to Bogotá after a long speaking tour and was looking forward to taking a little nap during the flight. The guy sitting next to me was a colorful character dressed in expensive clothes and sporting a large, gold chain around his neck. He was drinking whisky as fast as he could get the flight attendant to serve him. I wondered if I should try to say something to him but decided that he was too far gone, so I just shut my eyes and tried to sleep.

This, however, was not to be. The guy, being a little bit soused and wanting an audience, kept waking me up with one question after another. He insisted on finding out who I was and what I was doing in Colombia. When I told him I was a missionary, he turned white as a sheet, sobered up, and said that he had a confession to make.

It turned out that he had a wonderful wife and grown children in Miami, but now he was heading to Medellín to organize an apartment and shack up with a young girl. His family thought he was on a business trip.

He told me that he was not sure if God was for real or not, but just before he left, he started to have some serious misgivings about what he was doing. He said he felt like he had a little residue of faith left, so he prayed and asked God that if he was real, would he please send someone to tell him what God wanted him to do.

So I put my seat back up and sat there and told him exactly what the Lord thought about what he was planning to do and how stupid he was to even attempt to betray the wonderful family that God had given him.

The fellow began to weep and repent and said that when he got to Bogotá, he was going to turn around and catch the next plane back to Miami.

I never saw him again and do not know how it turned out in the end. The only thing I know is that God had an appointment for me to meet with him, and he was wide open to what I told him on behalf of the Lord.

When the Lord is leading us and we are operating in the nature of God, we do not have to make anything up; we do not have to force anything. All we have to do is flow with the opportunities that God places in our path.

> 16 *having a good conscience, so in that which they murmur against you as of evildoers, those that blaspheme your good conversation in the Christ may be confused.*

> 17 *For it is better (if the will of God so desires) that ye suffer for doing good than for doing evil.*

Many who are calling themselves Christians think they are doing something for the Lord, when in reality they are spiritually abusing people. If they suffer, it is because they are doing everything backwards.

Our life here on earth is full of pain and suffering, and this is unavoidable. But suffering for doing the will of God is so much better than suffering because of our own pride and arrogance.

> 18 *For the Christ also has once suffered for sins, the just for the unjust, that he might bring us to God, being put to death in the flesh, but made alive in spirit,*

19 *in which he also went and preached unto the imprisoned spirits,*

20 *which in the time past were disobedient, when once the patience of God waited in the days of Noah, while the ark was being made ready, wherein few, that is, eight souls were saved by water.*

21 *Unto the figure of which the baptism that does now correspond saves us (not taking away the uncleanness of the flesh, but giving testimony of a good conscience before God) by the resurrection of Jesus, the Christ,*

22 *who is at the right hand of God, having ascended into heaven, unto whom the angels and the authorities and powers are subject.*

What is the baptism that now corresponds and saves us? John the Baptist said:

Matthew 3

11 *I indeed baptize you in water unto repentance, but he that comes after me is mightier than I, whose shoes I am not worthy to bear; he shall baptize you in the Holy Spirit and fire,*

Paul wrote:

Ephesians 4

4 *There is one body and one Spirit, even as ye are called in one hope of your calling,*

5 *one Lord, one faith, one baptism,*

If there is only one baptism, what is *the baptism that does now correspond saves us (not taking away the uncleanness of the flesh, but giving testimony of a good conscience before God)?*

The one baptism that now corresponds and saves us is the baptism done by Jesus Christ into the Holy Spirit and fire. Baptism in water is only a symbol, and if Jesus does not intervene in our lives, we will not be saved.

Romans 5

10 *For if, when we were enemies, we were reconciled with God by the death of his Son, much more, now reconciled, we shall be saved by his life.*

Make no mistake. The only baptismal regeneration that can save us is when Jesus immerses us into new birth in his life, into the Holy Spirit and fire.

Maybe this is why Paul wrote:

1 Corinthians 1

17 *For Christ sent me not to baptize, but to preach the gospel,*

There is a clear witness by both Paul and Peter that the only work that will endure, the only work that can save us is that accomplished by the Lord Jesus Christ. If we surrender and submit to him, he desires to work in us and through us. This is the gospel.

1 Peter 3

19 *in which he also went and preached unto the imprisoned spirits,*

20 *which in the time past were disobedient, when once the patience of God waited in the days of Noah,*

while the ark was being made ready, wherein few,
that is, eight souls were saved by water.

Jesus even preached to the imprisoned spirits of those who had been disobedient in the days of Noah before the flood.

What happened with them?

What state are they in?

We do not know.

But we do know that after his death on the cross, Jesus descended into Hades, which was like a jail run by the Devil in which he had trapped the souls of virtually everyone who had died (Luke 16:22-24), and he preached to those who were imprisoned. He broke the power of death and took the keys of death and of Hades away from the Devil (Revelation 1:18) and ascended on high with those who were his (Ephesians 4:8-10).

Where am I going with this?

If Jesus even preached in Hades to the spirits of those who were disobedient from before the flood, we can rest assured that God knows how to conduct evangelism.

Therefore, what should we be doing?

The will of God. If we are to suffer, let it be according to the will of God.

Many people pray to the Lord and say something like this: *Lord, I am willing to serve you, except I do not want to do this, that, or the other thing, and I do not want to leave my home or my city or my country.*

When we pray like this, we set the parameters that the Lord must touch in our lives in order to bring us to maturity.

If we tell the Lord we are willing to serve him anywhere in the world except China, it will be impossible for us to get past a certain level of maturity until we are willing to go to China. Therefore, we may end up being disqualified from the fullness of the inheritance that God has set before us.

Peter goes over some important points. We are to have a clean conscience; we have to be willing to suffer according to the will of God, trusting that the Lord knows why this is necessary, and knowing that he will use the trials and tribulations we are facing to bring about great blessing. We can rest assured that the Lord will not allow anything to happen to us that is not according to his purpose (Romans 8:28).

Peter then compares this with *the baptism that does now correspond* and links it to Noah's ark.

Why?

Because it is baptism (immersion) into Jesus' death and into Jesus' resurrection life; and Noah's ark represents this reality. This was not some little recreational baptismal escapade in someone's backyard swimming pool. Everyone upon the earth died in the flood except for eight souls.

The eight souls who were saved went through a long ordeal as the ark tossed and turned for 150 days upon huge waves that completely remade the surface of the earth. It was like an endless, wild rollercoaster. If they had not done their work conscientiously and according to the exact plans given to them by God, the ark would have come apart in the terrible storm, and no one would have been saved. As it was, they were saved inside the ark while they passed through the most terrible storm in history, and at the same time they tended to hundreds of wild animals that God sent along for the ride!

The water baptism of John the Baptist unto repentance is one thing (and has been very significant to many). But the baptism that can only be accomplished by Jesus Christ into the Holy Spirit and fire is in quite another class. Peter says it ranks right up there with Noah's ark.

The goal of Jesus' baptism is to actually bring about the death of our ego, the death of our pride, and the death of the lusts of the flesh. It will submerge us into his resurrection life until we are dead to sins and fully alive in Christ.

Let us look at this from a different angle:

Colossians 2

8 *Beware lest any man spoil you through philosophy and vain deceit, after the traditions of men, according to the elements of the world, and not after Christ.*

We have mentioned that the traditions of men have become profoundly engrained in much of the Christian Church. Religious rites, rituals, and symbols have replaced reality in most places.

Later, Peter writes about these *elements* being on fire when the day of the Lord arrives.

Where does the judgment begin?

From the house of the Lord, and if we are born again, we are part of the real temple of God. For this reason, the judgment must begin with each one of us who is willing to enter into a covenant according to the manner and conditions of God.

What will the Lord do to us?

He will begin to refine us and pass us through the fire with the goal of purifying his nature in us like pure gold. Gold is a symbol of his nature, and he desires to remove all the dross from our lives. Passing through the trials and tribulations of this life is the only way to do this.

Peter makes it clear, however, that we may suffer along the road to blessing in the will of God, but some of us will also suffer as a result of wrongdoing (which is under the curse).

In this life, we are subject to pain and suffering. It is impossible to avoid. We must face all manner of injustice. It is part of life in a fallen world. We may respond to the circumstances of life in one manner or another. We may respond in the life of Christ or in the life of Adam. In Christ, we are able to overcome every test and every trial. In Christ, we are able to make it through any amount of tribulation, just as Noah and his family were able to make it through a storm and a flood that destroyed everyone else in the entire world.

Therefore:

> 8 *Beware lest any man spoil you through philoso-*
> *phy and vain deceit, after the traditions of men,*
> *according to the elements of the world, and not after*
> *Christ.*
>
> 9 *For in him dwells all the fullness of the Godhead*
> *bodily,*
>
> 10 *and ye are complete in him, who is the head of all*
> *principality and power.*
>
> 11 *In whom also ye are circumcised with the circum-*
> *cision made without hands, in putting off the body*
> *of the sins of the flesh by the circumcision of the*
> *Christ;*

The circumcision of Christ is also related to baptism. This occurs when the power of God enters our hearts and cuts the control of the flesh, so we are no longer under the compulsive impulse of wrong desires. Our hearts will be managed by the Spirit of God and by the desires of God.

> 12 *buried together with him in baptism, wherein*
> *also ye are risen with him through the faith of the*
> *operation of God, who has raised him from the*
> *dead.*
>
> 13 *And you, being dead in sins and the uncircumci-*
> *sion of your flesh, he has quickened together with*
> *him, having forgiven you all trespasses,*
>
> 14 *blotting out the bill of the decrees that was*

*against us, which was contrary to us and took it
out of the way, nailing it to his cross [Gr. Stauros
– "stake"],*

*15 and having spoiled the principalities and the
powers, he made a show of them openly, triumphing
over them in it.*

What did the Lord accomplish?

The principalities and powers of this world thought they had
finally trapped him, but as they thought they were finishing him
off, he triumphed over them. He spoiled them and took their
arms, their covering, their hostages, and he redeemed us. He
even captured the keys to death and to Hades (Revelation 1:18).

If we follow the same path that he took, we will pass through
the circumcision of the heart and receive the baptism of Christ.

How many Jews were circumcised in the flesh as little babies
on the eighth day according to the law, yet never received the
circumcision of the heart that is without hands?

How many Christians have been baptized in water (according to one formula or another) over the past two millennia, yet
have never received the baptism of Christ into the Holy Spirit
and fire? If the nature of God is not planted deep within our
being, and there has been no circumcision of the heart where
evil desires of the flesh are cut out, we are only playing a religious game.

How many people are running around in churches (or in
synagogues) who have been water baptized (or circumcised in
the flesh) but have had no change of heart, no evidence of the
nature of Christ in their lives?

Both Paul and Peter tell us we can discount the traditions
of men if our hearts have been circumcised, and we have been
baptized into the name (nature) of Jesus and have the real Holy
Spirit and fire.

*16 Let no one therefore judge you in food or in drink
or in respect of a feast day or of the new moon or of
the sabbath days,*

*17 which are a shadow of things to come, but the
body is of the Christ.*

If we operate in the nature of God in the body of Christ, we
are in another realm beyond the religious realm of rites and
rituals. In this position we are free to participate in a religious
ceremony or to abstain.

*18 Let no one govern you according to their own
will under pretext of humility and religion of angels,
intruding into those things which they have not seen,
vainly puffed up by their fleshly mind,*

Many religious people attempt to govern others according to
their own will under the pretext of humility and religion. Note
that this verse is mistranslated in many English Bibles.

*19 and not holding fast to the Head, from whom
all the body, fed and united by its joints and bonds,
grows in the increase of God.*

Who is our *Head*?

The Lord Jesus.

Each one who is born again will have a direct connection
with the Head as well as joints and bonds with other members
of the body.

*20 For if ye are dead with the Christ to the elements
of the world, why, as though living unto the world,
do ye decree rites,*

21 touch not; taste not; handle not?

*22 Which all perish with the using, because they are
the commandments and the doctrines of men,*

23 *which things have indeed a show of wisdom in*
will worship and humility and neglecting of the
body, but they have absolutely no value against the
appetites of the flesh.

Therefore, of what usefulness are the rites and commandments
and doctrines of men? They have absolutely no value against
the appetites of the flesh, yet they contribute to what Paul calls
will worship.

1 Peter 4

1 *Since the Christ has suffered for us in the flesh, be*
ye also armed with the same thought; for he that has
suffered in the flesh has ceased from sin.

Those who are preaching and participating in a gospel in which
no one has to suffer in the flesh will never cease from sin.

The true gospel will involve suffering in the flesh, but the
Lord will use these trials and tribulations to set us free from sin
and cut every evil thought and desire out of the depths of our
hearts. Then our hearts will no longer be pulled in the wrong
direction. We used to be slaves of sin; now we will be slaves of
righteousness (Romans 6:18-23). We will now be going in the
exact opposite direction.

Religious rites and practices can never produce this change.
Commandments and doctrines of men have absolutely no value
against the appetites of the flesh. They only serve to foster a sense
of guilt and shame as the appetites of the flesh run rampant.
This, in turn, feeds a vicious cycle of more ritual.

The feelings of guilt come because people continue to sin.
Then they try to rid themselves of their guilt complex by going
to a church service, paying their tithe, going to mass, going to
confession or counseling, or whatever.

The only way to cease from sin is to be willing to suffer in the flesh according to the will of God as we follow in the footsteps of Jesus along the way of the cross.

Let us pray:

Heavenly Father:

We ask that we may understand and experience what it is to truly be born again of water and of the Spirit so that we may receive nourishment from your Word.

Please send the sword of your truth to cut through all the ties and bonds that we have with the things and with the powers of this world. Please cut the control of our flesh and circumcise our hearts, so we will not be led astray by anyone.

We ask that we might receive the liberty of the Holy Spirit – liberty to do your will, liberty to be slaves of righteousness.

We ask this in the name of our Lord Jesus Christ. Amen.

CHAPTER 5

Sharing in the Suffering of Christ

1 Peter 4

*1 Since the Christ has suffered for us in the flesh, be
ye also armed with the same thought; for he that has
suffered in the flesh has ceased from sin,*

*2 so that now the time that remains in the flesh, he
might live, not unto the lusts of men, but unto the
will of God.*

*3 For it should suffice us that during the time past of
our life we had done the will of the Gentiles, when
we conversed in lasciviousness, lusts, drunkenness,
gluttony, orgies, and abominable idolatries.*

Peter identifies with the Gentiles in this passage. He recognizes that as a Jew without Christ, the appetites of his flesh were not dealt with by keeping the Jewish rites and the commandments of men. Peter understands that there is no difference between Jew and Gentile, and the only solution is for all of us to enter into the life of Christ by a new birth by the Spirit.

If we are one with Christ in his death and in his resurrection, we will also be one with Christ in his sufferings. Peter links the suffering with Christ with our old man (our old nature) that is nailed to the cross, so we will cease from sin. When God begins a work in us, he is able to finish it, and this work is not finished until the old man is completely dead. This is why Jesus said,

It is finished, as he died upon the cross and accomplished our redemption. For each one of us, the circumstances of our "cross" may be different, but God will use trials, tribulations, and pain (suffering in the flesh) to bring us to where we are dead to sins.

John 19

30 *When Jesus therefore had received the vinegar, he said, It is finished, and he bowed his head and gave the Spirit.*

Jesus had to die in order to give us his Spirit, and only by the power of the Holy Spirit are we able to put to death the deeds of the flesh and live (Romans 8:13).

1 Peter 4

4 *And it seems strange to those that speak evil of you, that ye do not run with them to the same unchecked dissolution;*

5 *the same shall give account to him that is ready to judge the living and the dead.*

6 *Because for this cause was the gospel preached also to those that are dead, that they might be judged in flesh according to men, but live in spirit according to God.*

Here Peter is making the case for preaching to those who are dead in trespasses and sin, because everyone will eventually be judged by Christ. Those who are born again and are alive will be judged, and those who are dead in sin will be judged. The gospel is preached to those who are not saved, so they may be *judged in flesh according to men, but live in spirit according to God.*

7 *But the end of all things is at hand; be ye, therefore, temperate and watch unto prayer.*

At the time that Peter wrote this, the siege of Jerusalem had probably begun. Peter knew by the teachings of Jesus and the Spirit that the temple would be completely destroyed, but God was building a new temple, built without hands, out of living stones.

Jesus said:

Matthew 5

17 *Think not that I am come to undo the law or the prophets; I am not come to undo, but to fulfil.*

18 *For verily I say unto you, Until heaven and earth pass away, not one jot or one tittle shall pass from the law until all is fulfilled.*

The Jews of Peter's day reaped the full consequences of their disobedience. Their only chance to escape was to desist from their own works and enter into Christ. Even so, God was patient and gave them a relatively long time to hear and respond to the gospel. About thirty years after the gospel was clearly sent to the Gentiles, starting with the house of Cornelius, armies surrounded Jerusalem, and the fate of the Jews was irrevocably sealed.

By the Spirit and from his own experience, Peter saw all of this coming. Therefore, we see the extreme importance of the next verse because we are also living in a time that is coming to an end. This time God will first separate the tares from among the wheat.

1 Peter 4

8 *And above all things have fervent charity among yourselves; for charity shall cover a multitude of sins.*

Charity is the love of God. It is unselfish and born of sacrifice. Charity (Gr. *Agape*) is redemptive by its very nature. Unless we are filled with the presence of God, we cannot experience this quality of love. For our human love (Gr. *Phileos*) is self-serving and tends to seek something in return, unless Christ has circumcised our hearts. Then it will be possible for us to:

> 9 *Lovingly be hospitable one to another without murmuring.*

> 10 *Let each one according to the gift that he has received, administer it unto the others, as a good steward of the diverse graces of God.*

> 11 *If anyone speaks, let him speak as the oracles of God; if anyone ministers, let them do it according to the virtue which God gives, that God in all things may be glorified through Jesus, the Christ, unto whom is glory and dominion for ever and ever. Amen.*

Notice that when we are born again, each one of us will be gifted by God and thereby have something important to contribute to the body of Christ. We are stewards of the diverse graces of God when we receive gifts from God, and we must take care to operate our God-given talents in the virtue which God gives. Virtue relates to the power of godly character.

Charity (the love of God which is unselfish and redemptive by its very nature) is a virtue that we can only obtain from the ongoing presence of God in our lives. Those who follow religion and commandments of men are like the scribes and Pharisees and priests of Peter's day. They will never obtain virtue unless they repent and radically change course. Peter lived to see the end result of the blindness and stubbornness of the Jewish religious leaders, as all things related to the age of the law came to a tragic end. The curse described in the book of Deuteronomy came suddenly upon them (Deuteronomy 32).

12 *Beloved, think it not strange when you are tried by fire (which is done to prove you) as though some strange thing happened unto you,*

13 *but rejoice, inasmuch as ye are partakers of the afflictions of the Christ, so that also in the revelation of his glory, ye may rejoice in triumph.*

The Christian Jews had been forced to flee Jerusalem with very little notice and were being scattered in the midst of intense persecution all across the known world, even as Peter was writing this. They had lost their houses and lands. Only those who, prompted by the Holy Spirit, had sold their property ahead of time and invested the proceeds in the work of the Lord converted their earthly riches into eternal gain.

14 *If ye are reproached for the name of Christ, blessed are ye; for the glory and the Spirit of God rests upon you; certainly on their part he is blasphemed, but on your part he is glorified.*

15 *So let none of you suffer as a murderer, or as a thief, or as an evildoer, or as desirous of the things of others.*

Jesus repeatedly described the rulers of natural Jerusalem (openly and in his parables) as being all of the above. Jesus said that they were sons of their father, the Devil, who was a murderer from the beginning of his rebellion against God (John 8:44).

16 *But if anyone suffers as a Christian, let him not be ashamed, but let him glorify God on this behalf.*

Remember this extremely important quality of God: He does not destroy the righteous along with the wicked. *For a just man falls seven times and rises up again, but the wicked shall fall into evil* (Proverbs 24:16).

17 *For it is time that the judgment begins from the*

*house of God; and if it first begins with us, what
shall the end be of those that do not obey the gospel
of God?*

*18 And if the righteous are saved with difficulty,
where shall the unfaithful and the sinner appear?*

*19 Therefore, let those that are afflicted according
to the will of God commit the keeping of their souls
unto him as unto a faithful Creator, doing good.*

These words are written to encourage us as we face the trials
and tribulations that surround us as we obey God.

1 Peter 5

*1 The elders who are among you I exhort (I am also
an elder with them and a witness of the afflictions
of the Christ, and also a participant of the glory that
shall be revealed).*

*2 Feed the flock of God which is among you, caring
for her, not by force, but willingly; not for shameful
lucre, but with willing desire;*

*3 and not as having lordship over the heritage of the
Lord, but in such a manner as to be examples of the
flock.*

*4 And when the great Prince of the pastors shall
appear, ye shall receive the incorruptible crown of
glory.*

The word *elder* means "older" and is of the same root as the
word *mature*. In Hebrew and in Greek, the word for *mature*
is the same word as for *perfection*. In the Old Testament, the
government of each town, village, tribe, or clan consisted of

the elders who would sit at the gate and deal with problems or conflicts whenever they surfaced.

In his letters to Titus and to Timothy, Paul describes the godly characteristics of elders. They are to be the husband of one wife. They are to have governed their household well. They are not to be given to excess wine, and so on. The problem comes when people read this and then attempt to select elders at their own discretion or by popular vote from the congregation. The New Testament is not law; it is grace. This means that the selection of elders and their fulfillment of that role will only work if God is in charge and is actively involved by way of the Holy Spirit.

Only God can bring someone to maturity in Christ. When this takes place, the good fruit of the Spirit is apparent to everyone who has discernment from God.

> 5 *Likewise, young people, be subject to the elders in such a manner that you are all subject to one another. Be clothed with humility of will, for God resists the proud and gives grace to the humble.*

> 6 *Humble yourselves, therefore, under the mighty hand of God, that he may exalt you in due time,*

> 7 *casting all your cares upon him, for he cares for you.*

If we are born from above, God is our Father and he has direct responsibility to discipline each and every one of his sons (and this does not refer to gender).

The real elders are not those who are immature (regardless of their age or the titles that may have been bestowed upon them by men). Elders are those who, by their example, by the evidence of the fruit of the Spirit in their lives, have authority from God to lead and shepherd others (primarily by giving a good example). The young people who are still immature are to be subject to their elders and to one another.

Some people ask, "What about women?"

Notice that Peter does not specify gender when he mentions elders or when he mentions young people, and his letter is addressed to the *strangers*, which consist of Jews and Gentiles who are one in Christ and scattered all over the world. Scripture also states that in Christ there is neither male nor female (Galatians 3:28). We see that the recipients of Peter's letter are not under Jewish order, which was being totally destroyed even as Peter wrote.

Under the Old Covenant, a woman could not directly enter into a covenant with God, because the sign of the covenant was circumcision, and it is biologically impossible to circumcise a woman in the biblical sense of the word. Women were required to keep silent even when Christians were still attending meetings in the synagogue (such as in Corinth where Timothy ministered for many years). They were to ask their questions in private to their husbands (1 Corinthians 14:34-35; 1 Timothy 2:11-12).

Under the New Covenant, however, the sign of the covenant is a circumcised heart, and Christ may accomplish this regardless of gender. In Christ, there is neither male nor female. Nevertheless, a line of command still exists in the family that goes from God to Christ to the husband to the wife to the children, even if the husband is not a Christian (1 Peter 3:1).

Peter is speaking to all of us when he says:

> 8 *Be temperate and vigilant because your adversary the devil, as a roaring lion, walks about, seeking whom he may devour,*

> 9 *resist him steadfast in the faith, knowing that the same afflictions are to be accomplished in the company of your brethren that are in the world.*

My father has always told me: "Son, the circumstances of life are not of the utmost importance; it is your reaction to them that will be long remembered."

We know for sure that if we take a stand for Jesus Christ, the Enemy will attack us. Our response to those attacks is of utmost importance. Our attitude in the face of adversity and affliction will often determine the outcome.

> 10 *But the God of all grace, who has called us unto his eternal glory by Jesus, the Christ, after ye have suffered a little while, he himself perfects, confirms, strengthens, and establishes you.*
>
> 11 *To him be glory and dominion for ever and ever. Amen.*

People cannot come to maturity in Christ (that is, become an elder in the biblical sense of the word) unless they have passed through trials, tribulations, and afflictions. God's plan is to bring all of us to maturity (to perfection in Christ). Therefore, women must not be excluded from coming to maturity in Christ under the New Covenant. The Lord may use women as he sees fit, and he definitely has great plans for his bride.

> 12 *By Silvanus, a faithful brother; (according to my reckoning), I have written briefly, exhorting, and testifying that this is the true grace of God in which ye stand.*

Peter is extremely clear: The New Covenant is not based on law, religious rites and rituals, or commandments of men. The New Covenant is based on Jesus Christ and the power of his grace. This is the true grace of God in which we stand.

> 13 *Those here at Babylon, chosen together with you, salute you and so does Mark, my son.*

14 *Greet one another with a kiss of charity. Peace be with you all that are in Jesus, the Christ. Amen.*

Babylon was a code name that the early Christians (who were under intense persecution) had for Rome. Peter wrote his two epistles at or near Rome not long before he was killed for the cause of Jesus Christ. The tone and content of this letter make it clear that Peter was not just concerned with revelation and truth. He is sharing the message that he personally lived and breathed for decades in the midst of many trials, tribulations, and afflictions. This is why this book comes forth with such powerful authority in the Lord.

Our own case is similar in that if we are to be effective ministers of the power and grace of God, we must have first-hand experience and revelation of the matters at hand. Those who sent Moses up to the mountaintop to hear the voice of God because they did not want to take any personal risk all died in the wilderness (Joshua 5:6). The Romans destroyed all those who refused to hear and receive Jesus, even though their temple and religion looked impressive from the outside.

As the day of the Lord dawns, the tables are going to turn, and the Lord says that he will remove the wicked from among the righteous (Matthew 13:49). He will not only cleanse his people, but he promises that he will continue his cleansing until there are new heavens and a new earth in which dwell righteousness (2 Peter 3:13).

Let us pray:

Heavenly Father:
We ask that we may be able to understand and put into practice your truths. We ask that the judgment that is soon coming upon the entire earth will not catch us by surprise. We ask that when judgment falls upon the world, we will have already been judged

because we submitted to your mighty hand. May we be among the righteous who with difficulty are saved because the trials, tribulations, and afflictions that we have suffered according to your will have brought forth excellent fruit in our lives. May you bring us to maturity in Christ.

We ask this in the name of our Lord Jesus Christ. Amen.

CHAPTER 6

A Foundation of Faith and Virtue

2 Peter 1

1 Simon Peter, slave and apostle of Jesus Christ, to those that have obtained like precious faith with us in the righteousness of our God and Saviour Jesus Christ:

Simon Peter declares himself to be a slave and apostle (or "sent one") of Jesus Christ. A slave has an owner.

This letter is addressed to those who have obtained like-precious faith with us. They obtained a faith that they did not previously have. If they already had it, they would not have had to obtain it.

The faith that we can obtain is the faith of Christ, for his faith can operate in us (Revelation 14:12).

We are all given a measure of faith (Romans 12:3-6), and if we have faith even like a tiny mustard seed, we can accomplish many things (Luke 17:6). Scripture speaks of faith that can move mountains and of the type of mountains that can be moved (Matthew 17:14-21).

Every type of enemy structure, every kingdom of man, and every demonic power that dominates the natural man (every mountain) can be removed with faith. When the Lord comes into our lives, he desires to change our hearts to take us to another mountain, the mountain of God where he desires for us to dwell with him in holiness.

Our faith is sufficient for us to trust him. Then he desires to live in us so his faith can produce an effect inside of us.

Two classes of faith are mentioned in the Bible: our faith and his faith. In order to overcome, we need him and his faith. Sometimes the word *faith* and the word *faithfulness* are the same in the original language. Either word is translated one way or the other according to context.

The Lord Jesus knew he was going to die on the cross, yet it was extremely difficult to get this across to the disciples, who were still fighting among themselves over who was the greatest.

Jesus' claims had a stunning effect on Simon Peter who found himself denying the Lord three times before the rooster crowed twice in the early morning of the day of the crucifixion. Peter never denied the Lord again, and he eventually martyred for the cause of Christ. The Lord had to break the apostles of their carnal mentality, and it took his death for this to happen. After the death and resurrection of Jesus, Peter understood exactly what Jesus had been trying to get him to understand.

On the other hand, Judas went past a point of no return and never made it to the resurrection. My father told me God would never waste a human life. He will always derive some benefit. If nothing else, he can always use someone as a bad example for everyone else! Such was the sad case with Judas.

The only way to make sure we do not meet with a similar fate is by having a covenant with the Lord. Then the Lord can correct us when we need it and intervene as he sees fit in the most intimate areas our lives. This way he can nip in the bud anything that he does not like and make sure we will never have a fatal problem.

Scripture states: *Then when lust has conceived, it brings forth sin; and sin, when it is finished, brings forth death* (James 1:15).

Peter denied the Lord three times. After his resurrection, Jesus restored Peter and gave him the opportunity to rectify this denial three times by declaring his love for the Lord. I believe we can have complete security in the Lord. In this second letter, Peter gives us a formula so we will never fall. Peter ought to know.

We may think that God is strict (and in a certain sense, he is). We may think that holiness is impossible for us (and this is correct). But what is impossible for us is not impossible for God (Mark 10:27).

> 2 *Grace and peace be multiplied unto you in the knowledge of God and of our Lord Jesus,*

My father's favorite definition of grace is that it is God doing for us what we are unable to do for ourselves. The law of multiplication is also important.

Note that this does not say grace and peace be *added* unto you.

Grace and peace can be multiplied unto us in the knowledge of God and of our Lord Jesus because the knowledge of God is infinite. God desires to unleash an infinite geometric progression of his grace and peace into us, as we submit to Jesus and allow him to live his life in and through us by the power of the Holy Spirit. His faith has no limits, and even faith like a grain of a mustard seed on our part can get this dynamic rolling.

Grace pertains to the power of God to change our lives. Grace is not a work of magic. True, we do not deserve God's grace and it is, therefore, unmerited favor. But the grace of God is the fruit of power, and the power of God is unlimited. There is also a special relationship between faith and grace.

By God's grace, he is able to not only forgive our sins, but also to cleanse us from all unrighteousness no matter what it takes to accomplish this. The unlimited resources of his grace and peace are available to us:

> 3 *as all things that pertain to life and to godliness are given us of his divine power, through the*

*knowledge of him that has called us by his glory and
virtue,*

Godliness relates to the very nature of God.

This is not saying that here upon this earth we only have
access to a small measure of the grace and goodness of God, or
that we only have enough grace to have our sins forgiven but
not enough to give us victory over sin. This Scripture does not
say we have to wait until we die and go to heaven to receive *all
things that pertain to life and to godliness.*

This Scripture directly implies that if we do not have enough
grace and peace, it is because we lack knowledge of him. This
is why many people have not experienced the multiplication
of the grace and peace of God in their lives.

Peace is much, much more than the absence of conflict.
The Hebrew word is *Shalom* and means that "nothing is lacking; complete rest and well-being." This is another word with
no limits and can reach into infinity in the knowledge of God
and of our Lord Jesus.

So Peter is going to share his secret with us of how to tap into
this unlimited provision for all of our needs. God has provided
for everything, but most Christians are limping along on a tiny
portion of the grace of God. Therefore, they have been unable
to enter into God's rest; they have been unable to enter their
inheritance in Christ and experience the unlimited depths of
the peace of God.

This peace hinges on the knowledge of him who has called
us by his glory and virtue,

> 4 *whereby are given unto us exceeding great and
> precious promises, that by these ye might be made
> participants of the divine nature, having fled the
> corruption that is in the world through lust.*

We are talking about nothing less than being made participants of the divine nature and therefore of unlimited potential. This change starts out like a seed planted in our hearts that we must receive by faith. The potential of the seed includes exceedingly great and precious promises in a realm where everything that relates to God is eternal and unlimited.

All of God's promises are conditional, and the first condition we see here is that it is absolutely essential that we have *fled the corruption that is in the world through lust*. This condition must be fulfilled in order for us to begin to receive the promise.

All of God's promises and all of his conditions have to do with the state of our heart. We cannot fulfill his conditions without a pure heart, and having a pure heart is impossible unless God has judged our being, the very depths of our heart.

Two types of judgment are described in Scripture: judgment with mercy and judgment without mercy. Jesus said, *Blessed are the merciful for they shall obtain mercy* (Matthew 5:7). He also said that if we forgive, we shall be forgiven (Matthew 6:14-15). These are two of the greatest promises in the Bible.

> 5 *Ye also, giving all diligence to the same, show forth virtue in your faith; and in virtue, knowledge;*
>
> 6 *and in knowledge, temperance; and in temperance, patience; and in patience, fear of God;*
>
> 7 *and in fear of God, brotherly love; and in brotherly love, charity.*
>
> 8 *For if these things are in you and abound, they shall not let you be idle nor unfruitful in the knowledge of our Lord Jesus Christ.*
>
> 9 *But he that lacks these things is blind and walks feeling the way with his hand, having forgotten that he was purged from his old sins.*

10 *Therefore, brethren, give all the more diligence to make your calling and election sure; for doing these things, ye shall never fall.*

11 *Because in this manner the entrance shall be abundantly administered unto you in the eternal kingdom of our Lord and Saviour Jesus Christ.*

This is a tremendous promise. Notice the progression:

5 *show forth virtue in your faith;*

As we have faith in him (depend on him), we will become more and more able to show forth virtue. Virtue comes only from God. Virtue is clean and pure and comes with power. Virtue accompanies the presence of God in us. Virtue is a work of grace and begins to accelerate the will of God in and through us. Many modern Bibles have eliminated this word, but here is a sample of how this word is used in the original:

Exodus 18

21 *Moreover thou shalt consider out of all the people men of virtue, such as fear God, men of truth, hating covetousness,*

Luke 6

19 *And the whole multitude sought to touch him, for there went virtue out of him and healed them all.*

When sick, unclean people touched Jesus, notice that he did not become unclean. The virtue in him overpowered their uncleanness, and all of them were healed.

Romans 15

19 *with power of signs and wonders, in virtue of the Spirit of God; so that from Jerusalem and round*

about unto Illyricum, I have filled the entire area
with the gospel of Christ.

Virtue of the Spirit of God is what brings about powerful signs and wonders.

1 Corinthians 4

20 *For the kingdom of God is not in words, but in*
virtue.

Revelation 12

10 *And I heard a loud voice saying in heaven, Now*
is come salvation and virtue and the kingdom of our
God and the power of his Christ; for the accuser of
our brethren is cast down, who accused them before
God day and night.

In his first epistle, Peter stated that God the Father has begotten us again unto a living hope by the resurrection of Jesus, the Christ, from the dead:

1 Peter 1

4 *unto the incorruptible inheritance that cannot be*
defiled and that does not fade away, conserved in
the heavens for you,

5 *who are kept in the virtue of God by faith, to*
attain unto the saving health which is made ready to
be manifested in the last time.

Virtue is the power of the character of God focused toward everything that is clean and healthy. It produces health and cleanliness and is linked to salvation. Virtue is God's remedy for evil desires and the lust of the flesh. Virtue is poison to the old, Adamic nature.

Notice that we are kept in the virtue of God by faith. If we wish to claim the promise of God (that we shall never fall), we must show forth virtue in our faith. Otherwise, faith without works is dead (James 2:17). The only works that matter are those accomplished in and through us by the virtue of God.

2 Peter 1

5 Ye also, giving all diligence to the same, show forth virtue in your faith; and in virtue, knowledge;

In other words, our faith can get us to the altar, but at the altar we need to enter into a covenant with the Lord so his life and his faith come forth in us. This is virtue. This will quicken our mortal body, change our heart, and effect a great cleansing of our entire being.

This quickening will be the beginning of a great dynamic, a great process of change as we walk with the Lord. Those who stop and begin to notice the wind and the waves instead of keeping their eyes fixed on the Lord will begin to sink. Peter knows about all kinds of things that can go wrong, so he continues to exhort us here to keep going on the path of faith and obedience to the Lord so we will never fall.

Therefore, we are to show forth virtue in our faith and in virtue, knowledge. Many religious seminaries and training institutions put the cart before the horse here. We are to add knowledge (science and mental learning) to the solid dynamic of faith and virtue. This is not the same as indoctrinating a religious proselyte. The church is full of how-to seminars, catechisms, premarital counseling, you name it; yet even if the teaching is solid, God says it must be conducted upon the right foundation and in the right dynamic. Otherwise, those who are educated with knowledge will become vain and proud (and pride goes before a fall).

Too much knowledge can be dangerous if it does not flow as a result of faith and virtue. This happened to Adam and Eve when they chose the Tree of the Knowledge of Good and Evil instead of trusting in God and allowing his virtue to flow in and through them. Only in the virtue of God will we ever be qualified to handle knowledge. If you do not believe me, just take a good look at the secular universities scattered across the globe. Many of them, like the Ivy League universities of the United States, started out with a much different focus than they have today.

If we have a solid base and a solid dynamic of faith and virtue, we will be able to get a sound education in the realm of knowledge. Peter was an uneducated fisherman, but notice the sublime wisdom from God that is flowing forth from him as he writes.

6 *and in knowledge, temperance;*

Temperance is another word that has been eliminated from many Bible translations, because it does not collaborate well with the religion of men, which tends to prohibit whatever it cannot control. Religion tends to condemn or condone; one thing is good, another is bad. What those who are merely religious decide is "good" can then be used without limits, and what they decide is "bad" is totally prohibited. This type of practice will eventually isolate a religious person from anyone who is not of his or her tight group or set. This makes it more and more difficult for them to reach the lost, and they become isolated more and more from unsaved family members. Temperance is what Jesus practiced when he ate and drank with the publicans and sinners.

Temperance means everything in its proper place and in the right measure according to the will of God without deficiency or excess. Temperance means having our appetites and our entire being under the control of the Spirit of God. A temperate person will be neither anorexic nor gluttonous. They will not be a teetotaler or a drunkard. Or, if God has prohibited them from touching any alcohol, they will not insist that everyone else be teetotalers.

In the realm of knowledge, a temperate person will not go overboard with theory and will not be deficient in practical experience. He will be in perfect balance; he will have perfect mental health and pursue only what the Holy Spirit indicates and according to the depth and intensity that he prescribes. Many things, items, or areas of knowledge are not necessarily good or evil in and of themselves; it just depends on how we use them. The Lord may deal differently from person to person and allow or even encourage someone else to do something that he does not allow me to do. And if I am not allowed to do something, that does not necessarily mean I should run around prohibiting everyone else from doing it. In order to be effective, temperance must spring from the heart of each individual who has been transformed by the power and virtue of God.

> 5 *show forth virtue in your faith; and in virtue, knowledge;*
>
> 6 *and in knowledge, temperance; and in temperance, patience;*

If the religion of men is short on temperance, patience will be almost completely missing. When God is dealing with each of us regarding temperance, we often attempt to apply what we are learning to the lives of others without waiting for God to work in their lives as he is working in ours.

The tendency of man (and of religion influenced by man) is to distill principles from the Scriptures and blindly apply them without the wisdom of God. The secular world seems convinced that it can solve major problems simply by legislating new laws.

Yet it is oblivious to the fact that each individual desperately needs a change of heart.

The religion of men does not trust the feelings of the heart. Men want to be mentally led by spiritual and moral principles that they see as cut-and-dried. But if the Lord is working in our hearts with his virtue and is bringing forth knowledge of him and the mind of Christ, the New Covenant will be active in us. He will write his laws on the tablet of our hearts and in our minds. Our feelings and thoughts are not reliable, but his are!

Those who think they must begin with knowledge in their rush to indoctrinate do not even begin with the right kind of knowledge, because they get their directives from one another instead of from God. (This is spiritual homosexuality, and it will always be sterile; it can never bring forth new life.) They cultivate the knowledge of good and evil from their own minds and according to their own interpretation of Scripture and then share this with one another.

The saddest part of this is that it quenches the Holy Spirit. The freedom and liberty of the Spirit is restricted and reduced in the midst of a flurry of doctrine, rules, and regulations. Religious people will not even allow God to correct their decrees. The Pharisees were furious at Jesus for healing people on the Sabbath, because this did not fit with their rules and with their doctrine.

Or after we have decided that something is okay, that it is benign, this may not really be the case in God's eyes. If our new house or our new car or our new job is competing for first place in our lives, then these things may become idols to us. We need temperance in all things. As we walk with him, the Lord will temper us so we can live in the world but not be of the world, so we can participate in all the blessings that he bestows upon us without any religious sense of guilt.

The idea of temperance goes against the grain of religion

according to the ways of men, but it is life according to the ways of God, according to the divine nature.

> 5 *show forth virtue in your faith; and in virtue, knowledge;*

> 6 *and in knowledge, temperance; and in temperance, patience; and in patience, fear of God;*

To be patient is to not be in a rush to precipitate action on our own or judge a given situation, until we have clearly heard from the Lord. As God works in our lives, the Scripture states that he is patiently waiting for good fruit to come to maturity in us.

Some people refuse to make decisions because they are afraid of the potential consequences. Let us not confuse this with patience. Young army officers who are being trained for battle are taught that when under fire in a difficult situation, any decision they make will be better than making no decision at all. Any dithering allows the enemy to overwhelm them.

We are to show forth in our patience the fear of God. The fear of the Lord is the beginning of wisdom. We need to make sure that before we make a move (even in temperance), it is okay with God. Otherwise, we must sit still and be patient until we know what is the mind of Christ regarding the matter. Sometimes God gives us complete freedom regarding a matter. This will happen more and more as we approach maturity, but he always reserves the right to intervene and check us. When this happens, we must wait patiently until he releases us to continue.

If we are patient in the fear of God, he will show us everything we need to know. He will zero in on every little detail of our lives. Every thought will be brought captive to Christ. He will order all our ways. For when the ways of the righteous are pleasing to the Lord, he even causes our enemies to come and be at peace with us (Proverbs 16:7). I have experienced this many times.

If we are patient in the fear of God, he will refine us and fine-tune us so everything we do is pleasing to him. He will work on every little detail as we come to maturity in Christ. As the fruit of the Holy Spirit comes forth in us, things get more interesting because the seed is in the fruit. Now God will be able to use us to help plant the gospel and feed those who hunger and thirst for righteousness.

The old man in the old nature can never be satisfied or feel fulfilled, because the appetites and ambitions of the old man are insatiable. It does not matter how much money he obtains or how many properties he owns or how much he eats or drinks; he will never, ever be satisfied.

Jesus says *Blessed are those who hunger and thirst for righteousness for they shall be satisfied* (Matthew 5:6). Righteousness only comes from God. Apart from God, man can only come up with self-righteousness.

A brother came up to me and said he wanted to be unselfish and do something for the Lord. He offered to provide us with some fence posts that we needed. Everything was going fine until he billed us double the going commercial rate. Still, we are to respond to situations like this in temperance and with patience in the fear of God until we know the mind of Christ.

However, these types of situations are not what is most important; the most important thing is what is going on in our hearts. Jesus says that the person who is unfaithful with little will be unfaithful with much, and the person who is faithful with little can be trusted with more responsibility.

Sometimes God gives us an opportunity, and we do not do so well the first time around. Yet in his mercy, God is easy on us and prepares us for another opportunity to see if we will be more diligent the second time around.

Some people have never been able to receive the true spiritual treasures, because they have never been proven faithful according to the ways of the Lord with earthly things.

In our patience, we are to show forth our fear of God. We are to remain steady and calm in any situation until we know the mind of Christ in the matter. Many things and various factors are intertwined in our lives and in how we relate to others. God does not want us to be doing things that are extreme or borderline, nor does he desire for us to be complacent and unresponsive. He desires for us to be in the center of his will. This is precisely what Peter was writing about.

> 5 *show forth virtue in your faith; and in virtue, knowledge;*
>
> 6 *and in knowledge, temperance; and in temperance, patience; and in patience, fear of God;*
>
> 7 *and in fear of God, brotherly love; and in brotherly love; charity.*

In our fear of God, we are to show forth brotherly love.

Many people fear God and believe that the things of God are so sacred and sublime that these people can be incredibly hard on those who do not live up to their standards.

Jesus said we are to love the Lord our God with all our heart and all our soul and all our might, and that we are also to love our neighbor as ourself. He also said that it is impossible for us to love God whom we cannot see if we do not love our brother whom we can see.

In our brotherly love we are to show forth charity, which is the redemptive love of God.

Our brotherly love (Gr. *Phileos*) for those around us needs to be tempered with the love of God (Gr. *Agape*). Otherwise, self-interest can creep in. Our love for children, parents, or siblings can be cruel and manipulative if we do not have a big dose of the sacrificial, redemptive love of God.

If we have been given responsibility to help care for the flock of God, we need to have more than brotherly love and affection for God's sheep. If we are to be true shepherds, we must also be willing to lay down our life for the sheep as Jesus did.

> 8 *For if these things are in you and abound, they shall not let you be idle nor unfruitful in the knowledge of our Lord Jesus Christ.*

How many Christians do you know who are idle and unfruitful in their knowledge of our Lord Jesus Christ?

Unfruitful means they are sterile and they are not producing spiritual offspring. They are sheep that do not reproduce.

If all these wonderful attributes that Peter has been writing about are in us and abound, we will become involved and productive in the kingdom of God. This means that what the Lord has planted in us will bear fruit and will be able to be planted into the lives of others and multiplied by the grace of God.

Sadly, our modern church has known very little about the power of multiplication. The word *multiplication* is another word that has been removed from some modern Bible translations by those who do not really believe it is possible for God to multiply his grace and his peace unto us without limits.

> 9 *But he that lacks these things is blind and walks feeling the way with his hand, having forgotten that he was purged from his old sins.*

Some people believe they can hear the voice of God and this is all they need. But they are in error, because those who can hear in the realm of the Spirit are blind if they cannot see in the realm of the Spirit as well.

Peter says that when these certain key things are lacking in the lives of believers, then these believers are spiritually blind and are merely walking along and feeling their way with their hands. Scripture also says that without vision the people perish (Proverbs 29:18).

This all relates to the status of each heart because Jesus said, *Blessed are the pure in heart, for they shall see God* (Matthew 5:8).

The person who has no spiritual vision (even if they can hear the voice of God) will tend to be idle and unfruitful regarding the kingdom of God.

The work they are doing is not what God is really doing, even though it looks like they are involved in a great ministry. They could be producing spiritual bastards instead of fathering true spiritual sons of God.

This is serious business and, therefore, Peter gives a sound warning:

> 10 *Therefore, brethren, give all the more diligence to make your calling and election sure; for doing these things, ye shall never fall.*

Peter knows what it is like to sink; he knows what it is to be blindsided by temptation and deny the Lord; and he also knows how to make sure this will never, ever happen again. We need to listen to him. We need to make sure we appropriate this wonderful promise from God.

It is obvious here that the spiritual capacity to see with clarity is indispensable if we desire not to fall.

What will be the fate of all those "Christians" who claim to hear the voice of God and yet are blind to the spiritual realm? Jesus said that the religious leaders are like the blind leading the blind and they are all going to fall into a pit (Matthew 15:12-14).

What pit?

The bottomless pit of the insatiable desires of the natural man. The Devil will tell them how to use the things of God to get what they want in the earthly realm, and they will believe they hear the voice of God and will fall into the trap. Occasionally, they may really identify the voice of God, but it will tend to be hit-or-miss.

In order to see, we must participate in the divine nature and allow God to replace our old, stony heart with his soft, sensitive heart.

Due to the fact that blind "Christians" cannot see (and this is an issue of the heart), they are not able to discern what voice is speaking to them out of the spiritual realm. Under the law, special consideration was given for a blind person, but since the scribes and Pharisees claimed they could see, Jesus told them their guilt remained (Leviticus 19:14; John 9:39-41).

Some religious people are so confused that when the Devil tells them how to prosper in the things of this world (how to have their cake and eat it too), they think they are hearing the voice of God. And when God tells them that in order to follow Christ they must deny themselves, take up their cross, and pass through trials and tribulations, they think they are hearing the voice of the Devil.

These are those who are always insisting that God told them this and God told them that, but their lives never demonstrate the fruit of righteousness, even though they may have big testimonies and tell long stories.

Peter wrote about doing things God's way. God's way is a narrow gate with many trials, tribulations, and obstacles. We must pay attention:

> 11 *Because in this manner the entrance shall be abundantly administered unto you in the eternal kingdom of our Lord and Saviour Jesus Christ.*

Peter says that if we pay attention and do the things he is writing to us about, we shall never fall.

Scripture mentions those who were saved, but all of their works were burnt up (1 Corinthians 3:11-15).

> 12 *For this reason, I will not leave off reminding you always of these things, although ye know them and are established in the present truth.*

If you have read this far, there is a very good possibility that you are also established in the present truth. Even so, it is important to be constantly reminded. In the highest sense, the Lord Jesus is this present truth, for he is the way, the truth, and the life, and he is with us in his Spirit. What Peter was writing about so long ago continues to be *present truth*.

> 13 *Because I have the right (as long as I am in this tabernacle) to stir you up by reminding you,*

> 14 *knowing that shortly I must put off this my tabernacle, even as our Lord Jesus Christ has declared unto me.*

Peter was going to be crucified, and he already knew that the time of his departure was close. Therefore, he desired to hammer home *the present truth* addressed to:

2 Peter 1

> 1 *those that have obtained like precious faith with us in the righteousness of our God and Saviour Jesus Christ:*

Please take note that these promises, warnings, and admonitions are addressed to born-again Christians.

> 15 *I will also make sure with diligence that after my decease ye might remember these things.*

This is why Peter wrote this letter. He wanted to remind us of this present truth.

16 *For we have not made known unto you the power and coming of our Lord Jesus Christ, following cunningly devised fables, but as eyewitnesses of his majesty.*

Peter not only related what he heard, but also what he saw.

In order to be fruitful and productive for God, spiritual vision is indispensable.

Peter went up the mountain with Jesus and saw the transfiguration; he saw the glory of God and the fullness of the kingdom of God.

Now God desires to show forth his glory in us. In order to do this, he must open our spiritual eyes.

17 *For he received from God the Father honour and glory, when there came such a voice to him from the excellent glory, This is my beloved Son, in whom I am well pleased.*

18 *And we heard this voice which came from heaven, when we were together with him in the holy mount.*

It is interesting to note that in this testimony, first they saw the glory of God, and then they heard the voice.

When one sees with the vision that God gives, with the prophetic vision of God, and then God speaks, we can identify the speaker beyond the shadow of a doubt.

19 *We have also the most sure word of the prophets, unto which ye do well that ye take heed, as unto a light that shines in a dark place, until the day dawns and the morning star arises in your hearts,*

Who or what is the *morning star*?

Revelation 22

16 I AM the root and the offspring of David and the bright and morning star.

In the highest sense, the *morning star* is the Lord Jesus, but it is also the fullness of Christ revealed in his overcoming bride.

Revelation 2

26 And he that overcomes and keeps my works unto the end, to him will I give power over the Gentiles;

27 and he shall rule them with a rod of iron; as the vessels of a potter they shall be broken to shivers, even as I received of my Father.

28 And I will give him the morning star.

2 Peter 1

20 understanding this first, that no prophecy of the scripture is of any private interpretation.

21 For the prophecy did not come in times past by the will of man, but the holy men of God spoke being inspired by the Holy Spirit.

The prophecy may be interpreted as many times and on as many levels as God sees fit, and no one may give his own private interpretation. Just as the Holy Spirit inspired the prophecy, so must the interpretation also be inspired.

Therefore, God may apply a prophecy to Israel and then may apply the same prophecy to the church or to the end times. The Lord does not have any limit to the number of situations to which he may decide to apply a given prophecy.

2 Peter 2

*1 But there were also false prophets among the
people, even as there shall be false teachers among
you, who covertly shall bring in destructive sects and
shall deny the Lord that bought them, bringing upon
themselves swift destruction.*

Swift destruction could also have been translated *accelerated
perdition.*

At the beginning of this letter is the promise of grace and
peace being multiplied unto those established in the present
truth. Here we have swift judgment (or accelerated perdition)
for false prophets and false teachers.

*2 And many shall follow their pernicious ways,
by reason of whom the way of truth shall be
blasphemed.*

This has certainly happened over the past millennia since Peter
wrote these words.

*3 and in covetousness they shall make merchandise
of you with feigned words, upon whom the condemnation from a long time ago does not delay, and
their perdition does not sleep.*

This can easily happen to those who claim to see and yet are
blind. They launch themselves into ministry (or are launched
by some group or organization because they have completed
an approved curriculum or training course) instead of being
sent into ministry by the Lord. They are also the ones making
merchandise of (exploiting) those who are precious to the Lord.

Lucifer sinned in this way when he attempted to elevate
himself to a higher position than what God had authorized. He
was out for personal gain and made merchandise of Adam and

Eve. When he secured the dominion of the earth, one-third of the heavenly host followed him.

> 4 *For if God did not forgive the angels that sinned, but cast them down into the deepest abyss [Gr. Tartarus] and delivered them into chains of darkness, to be reserved unto judgment;*

> 5 *and if he did not forgive the old world, but kept Noah, a preacher of righteousness, with seven other persons, bringing in the flood upon the world of the ungodly;*

> 6 *and if he condemned by destruction the cities of Sodom and Gomorrha, turning them into ashes, making them an example unto those that after should live without fear and reverence of God;*

> 7 *and delivered just Lot, who was persecuted by those abominable people because of their nefarious conversation;*

Lot went down in God's book as a righteous person because he was conflicted as he watched all that was happening around him in Sodom. He was not living in the best place he could have chosen, and the decision to live there seriously affected his family. Even so, the Lord showed him great mercy.

> 8 *(for that righteous man dwelling among them, in seeing and hearing, afflicted his righteous soul from day to day with the deeds of those unjust people);*

In the day of Ezekiel, when the temple was full of abominations and the leadership of the people of God had gone completely off the rails, God put a mark on everyone who sighed and cried out against the evil that had dominated Israel. In the ensuing judgment, everyone who had the mark of God was spared (Ezekiel 9:4-6).

9 *the Lord knows how to deliver the godly out of
temptations and to preserve the unjust unto the days
of judgment to be punished;*

10 *and chiefly those that walk after the flesh in the
lust of uncleanness and despise dominion; presump-
tuous, arrogant, they are not afraid to speak evil of
the higher powers;*

11 *whereas even the angels, who are greater in
power and might, bring no curse of judgment
against them before the Lord.*

How many of those who have postulated themselves for ministry
(because inside they really despise the dominion delegated by
God) proliferate judgments against the Devil and his demons?
Those who do this then begin to give orders to the angels of
God. They have no idea what they are getting themselves into.

These people really believe in their own dominion and
therefore seek covering from some well-known leader or group.
This will avail them nothing.

12 *But these, speaking evil of the things that they do
not understand (as natural animals without reason, who are made to be taken and destroyed), shall
utterly perish in their own corruption,*

13 *receiving the reward of their unrighteousness, as
those that count it pleasure to live luxuriously every
day. These are spots and blemishes, who eat together
with you, while at the same time they revel in their
deceit,*

14 *having their eyes full of adultery, and not knowing how to cease from sin, baiting the unstable souls,
having their heart exercised in covetous practices;
cursed sons,*

Jesus is coming back for a bride without spot or wrinkle or any such thing. Therefore, he will remove the wicked from among the righteous.

> 15 *who forsaking the right way have erred, having followed the way of Balaam the son of Beor, who loved the wages of unrighteousness,*

> 16 *and was rebuked for his iniquity; a dumb animal accustomed to a yoke (upon which he was seated), speaking with man's voice, hindered the madness of the prophet.*

The problem with Balaam was not that his prophecies did not come true; the problem was that he loved the wages of unrighteousness. Tragically, he was one of the first casualties in the war.

> 17 *These are wells without water, clouds that are brought by a whirlwind, to whom gross darkness is reserved for ever.*

> 18 *For speaking arrogant words of vanity, they allure through the lusts of the flesh, through much wantonness, those that were clean escaped from those who converse in error,*

> 19 *promising them liberty, being they themselves the slaves of corruption: for he who is overcome by someone is subject to bondage by the one that overcame him.*

> 20 *Certainly, if having separated themselves from the contaminations of the world, by the knowledge of the Lord and Saviour Jesus Christ, they again entangle themselves therein and are overcome, their latter end is made worse for them than the beginnings.*

21 *For it would have been better for them not to have known the way of righteousness, than, after they have known it, to turn back from the holy commandment delivered unto them.*

22 *But it has happened unto them according to the true proverb, The dog returns unto his own vomit, and the sow that was washed to her wallowing in the mire.*

We need to recognize the seriousness of having knowledge of God and of the way of righteousness without the foundation of faith and virtue.

The Lord Jesus died as a consequence of obedience to God. His clean, victorious, and overcoming life, death, and resurrection won him the right to judge everyone (righteous and unrighteous). In addition to this, he is the Creator of everything. Therefore, he recovered the dominion that Adam lost to the Devil.

Those who love him also love his nature and his way of doing things. These two letters that Simon Peter wrote towards the end of his life make this clear.

We must allow God to work in us so he can change us and transform our being. This is the only way to ensure that we will not be trapped in a religious system of men, but will be able to follow and continue in the dynamic of being led by the authentic Spirit of God. He may take us through serious trials, tribulations, and afflictions, but we will gain a pure heart, for he will place his heart in us. Jesus said that the pure in heart shall see God.

Those who attempt to follow the Lord and are not concerned with purity of heart will end in terrible defeat.

Peter, therefore, having made it through many serious trials and temptations, exhorts us to give all diligence to:

5 show forth virtue in your faith; and in virtue, knowledge;

6 and in knowledge, temperance; and in temperance, patience; and in patience, fear of God;

7 and in fear of God, brotherly love; and in brotherly love; charity.

We are promised that this is the way to become fruitful and productive for God. If we do these things, we shall never fall. May God grant us the grace to make this happen.

Let us pray:

Heavenly Father:

We ask that this message may become a reality in our lives and that we may become your ambassadors. May we demonstrate a better way to those in the world around us – your way.

May we bear your presence, for we know that your presence radiates grace and peace. May your grace and peace be multiplied in and through us into a dying world.

We ask this in the name of the Lord Jesus Christ. Amen.

CHAPTER 7

Patience of a Thousand Years

2 Peter 3

*1 Beloved, I now write unto you this second epis-
tle, in which I alert with exhortation your pure
understanding,*

May this be the case with each of us, because only those
of pure understanding will really understand this
book. In order to have pure understanding we need to have a
pure heart.

*2 that ye keep in memory the words which were
spoken before by the holy prophets and of our commandment, that we are apostles of the Lord and
Saviour,*

*3 knowing this first, that there shall come in the last
days scoffers, walking after their own lusts*

*4 and saying, Where is the promise of his coming?
For since the day in which the fathers fell asleep, all
things continue as they were from the beginning of
the creation.*

Things will definitely not continue as they are. Even now, some
of the "scoffers" are realizing that the present state of things is
unsustainable here on planet earth. The reference to the *last
days* means the last days of the prophetic week. Peter gives
the key definition for this later in verse 8 when he states that

before the Lord one day is as a thousand years. Peter is living at the beginning of the fifth day, and he knows that there will be two more days (two thousand years) until the beginning of the day of the Lord (the seventh day). In verse 18, he mentions the day of eternity in which the new heavens and the new earth continue forever.

> 5 *Of course, they willingly ignore that the heavens were created of old and the earth standing out of the water and in the water, by the word of God;*
>
> 6 *by which the world that then was, being over-flowed with water, perished;*
>
> 7 *but the heavens, which are now, and the earth are conserved by the same word, kept unto the fire in the day of judgment and of perdition of the ungodly men.*

The heavens are described in Genesis 1:8 as a firmament that separated the waters above from the waters below. God opened the windows of heaven and the fountains of the deep to cause the great flood (Genesis 7:11).

The heavens, which are now like a veil that separates the people of God upon the earth from the direct presence of God, are like the veil between the Holy Place and the Holy of Holies in the temple. When this veil (the heavens) is removed, the earth will be judged by fire.

Just as the ancient world was judged by water, Peter prophesies that our present world will be judged by fire, which will consume both the heavens and the earth. In the great flood of Noah's day, the planet was not destroyed, but the ancient world or system was completely destroyed, along with all the wicked, and the face of the earth was remade.

Remember that in the Bible the word *earth* is a code word for Israel and the church, as opposed to the *sea*, which refers to the unconverted Gentiles, the realm of lost humanity. In Noah's day, the judgment only affected the men and animals inhabiting the dry land, but the judgment did not affect the creatures of the sea.

Scripture is clear that fire does not destroy everything. Gold, silver, and precious stones will not burn in the fire of judgment. The wood, hay, and stubble will be burnt up (Malachi 4:1; 1 Corinthians 3:11-13). In the book of Revelation, the judgment begins first upon the earth (upon the land), and then the sea is judged.

> 8 *But, beloved, be not ignorant of this one thing,*
> *that one day before the Lord is as a thousand years,*
> *and a thousand years are as one day.*

The plan of God is prefigured in Genesis according to the seven days of the week. Six one-thousand-year prophetic days have transpired since the creation of Adam. We are now entering the seventh prophetic day, which is referred to by the holy prophets and the apostles as the day of the Lord. Some think that this last day is the millennium and that it will also last for a thousand literal years (Revelation 20). Before the Lord, however, one thousand years are also as a day. Therefore, the day of the Lord can be however long he decides that it should be, as when Joshua commanded the sun and the moon to stand still until the victory over the enemies of God was won (Joshua 10:12-14).

> 9 *The Lord is not late concerning his promise, as*
> *some count lateness, but is patient with us, not will-*
> *ing that any should perish, but that all should come*
> *to repentance.*

Patience is a virtue included in the nature of God. God is not willing that any should perish. His emphasis is on how many can be saved, not on how many will perish.

> 10 *But the day of the Lord will come as a thief in*

the night, in which the heavens shall pass away with a great noise, and the elements, burning, shall be dissolved, and the earth and the works that are in it shall be burned up.

Isaiah 51

6 Lift up your eyes to the heavens, and look upon the earth beneath; for the heavens shall vanish away like smoke, and the earth shall wax old like a garment, and those that dwell therein shall perish in like manner; but my saving health shall be for ever, and my righteousness shall never perish.

Revelation 6

12 And I saw when he had opened the sixth seal, and, behold, there was a great earthquake; and the sun became black as sackcloth of hair, and the moon became as blood;

An earthquake is prophetic language for a great move of God. The sun represents the prosperity of this world. The moon represents Israel and the church.

13 and the stars of heaven fell upon the earth, even as a fig tree casts her figs, when she is shaken of a mighty wind.

The stars of heaven represent principalities and powers of authority in the heavens. Scripture states that the events concerning the second coming of Jesus Christ will shake the heavens and the earth (Isaiah 13:13; 24:17-23; Haggai 2:6-9; Hebrews 12:25-29).

14 And the heaven departed as a scroll when it is rolled together; and every mountain and island were moved out of their places.

Mountains and islands represent every fortress, stronghold, and private kingdom of religious humanism among the people of God.

> 15 *And the kings of the earth and the princes and the rich and the captains and the strong and every slave and every free man hid themselves in the caves and among the rocks of the mountains*
>
> 16 *and said to the mountains and to the rocks, Fall on us and hide us from the face of him that is seated upon the throne and from the wrath of the Lamb;*
>
> 17 *for the great day of his wrath is come, and who shall be able to stand before him?*

Those who dwell upon the earth are not the same as those who have made God their habitation. Those who dwell in the secret place of the Most High under the shadow of the Almighty (Psalm 91) will have nothing to fear when Jesus Christ is revealed from heaven in the day of the Lord. Any other covering will fail.

2 Peter 3

> 11 *Seeing then that all these things shall be dissolved, what manner of persons ought ye to be in all holy conversation and godliness,*
>
> 12 *waiting for and desiring earnestly for the coming of the day of God, in which the heavens being on fire shall be dissolved, and the elements shall melt with fervent heat?*

The use of the word *elements* in Scripture is very intriguing. It always relates to the underpinnings of the world (the system run by Satan) that cause humanity to be enslaved. We are all born into this world as slaves.

Galatians 4

3 *Even so we, when we were children, were in slavery under the elements of the world,*

2 Peter 3

13 *Nevertheless we, according to his promises, wait for new heavens and a new earth, in which dwells righteousness.*

14 *Therefore, beloved, seeing that ye hope for such things, be diligent that ye may be found of him in peace, without spot and blameless.*

15 *And have as saving health the patience of our Lord, even as our beloved brother Paul also according to the wisdom given unto him has written unto you*

16 *in almost all his epistles, speaking in them of these things, among which are some things that are hard to understand, which those that are ignorant and unstable twist, as they do also the other scriptures, unto their own destruction.*

Those who attempt to interpret the Scriptures in their own human wisdom will twist them around to their own destruction, because they will fail to heed the warnings. They always think that the warnings are for someone else. This happens because they are ignorant and unstable, always trying to figure out a way to save their own lives, instead of being willing to lose their lives for the sake of the Lord and of the gospel.

17 *Ye, therefore, beloved, seeing ye know these things in advance, be on guard lest by the error of the*

*wicked ye be deceived with the others and fall from
your own steadfastness.*

*18 But grow in grace and in the knowledge of our
Lord and Saviour, Jesus Christ. To him be glory both
now and until the day of eternity. Amen.*

These two short books are Peter's last instruction and warning
to the scattered believers. He reminds us that after being born
again of incorruptible seed, we are sent by God to build the
body. He encourages us to submit our will to God, replacing
our will with his, and through obedience obtain a pure heart.
Being cleansed from the inside out sets us free from sin to be
slaves of righteousness. We become the living stones of the
temple with Christ as the Head.

As living stones, grace and peace can be multiplied to us as
we become partakers of the divine nature. We are no longer
held to laws, religious rites, or rituals. Where religion condemns
and condones, God's grace frees us to serve him. From our trials and tribulations, we will triumph into maturity, which is
where Peter is urging us to go.

Let us pray:

Heavenly Father:
*We ask that we might understand the urgency of this message,
as your day is close upon us. May we prepare our hearts, may we
have pure hearts, may we allow your government in our hearts
until we are completely cleansed.*

We ask this in the name of our Lord Jesus Christ. Amen.

About the Author

Russell Stendal, a former hostage of Colombian rebels, is a life-long missionary to that same group in the jungles of Colombia. He is an influential friend to military and government leaders in Colombia, Cuba, Mexico, Venezuela, and the United States. Russell's ministry shares the gospel via twelve radio stations, hundreds of thousands of Bibles, books, and movies distributed through airplane parachute drops, and numerous speaking engagements for groups of leaders, prisoners, and individuals. Russell goes wherever the Lord leads, whether it's to speak with a president or to go deep into the jungle to help an individual in trouble. He has witnessed thousands commit their lives to Christ.

Russell and his coworkers have built dozens of radio stations in Latin America that concentrate a clear message on remote and dangerous areas where persecution of Christians is rampant. More than 120,000 Galcom solar-powered radios have been deployed to those being discipled. Most of the programming is in Spanish, but they also transmit in almost a dozen native languages where a great move of God is presently taking place. Russell  preaches through the Bible, a chapter or so per message. More than 1,000 messages have been recorded and aired repeatedly. The chapters of this book are samples of these messages preached on the radio in the Colombian war zone about ten years ago. The key website is www.fuerzadepaz. com. Pray for Russell and his team as they expand Spanish-language radio coverage into places like Cuba, Venezuela, Mexico, and Central America.

Plans are in the works for new stations broadcasting in English that will provide coverage into Africa (where there are over 300 million English speakers) and possibly even into Asia and the Middle East. The first stage, as the programming is refined, will be Internet radio. After that, we want to begin shortwave radio transmission and distribution of Galcom radios in Africa and elsewhere as God opens the doors. The new radios have digital audio Bibles on board, and the goal is to move in the direction of digital shortwave transmissions within the next few years.

Connect with Russell's Ministry

Website

www.cpcsociety.ca

Receive newsletter updates

http://goo.gl/amBsCD

Buy books

http://amzn.to/1nPLcNL

God's Plan for **Spiritual**
Battle

Victory over Sin, the World, and the Devil

Russell M. Stendal

I love a good fight. When unjustly attacked, I have learned to seek the guidance and leadership of the Holy Spirit and retaliate by Overcoming Evil with Good. There is a huge difference between a Peacemaker and a Pacifist!

This Battle Plan for spiritual warfare, gleaned from the life and message of Jesus, especially the Sermon on the Mount and the Beatitudes, was on my heart even before I was kidnapped by terrorists and held hostage under extreme conditions in 1983. Since then, thousands of missionaries, pastors, and other Christians have been kidnapped, murdered, or forced to flee from their places of ministry in rural Colombia. Had these Christians known and understood this battle plan for spiritual warfare, they could have been victorious instead of prematurely suffering defeat.

Many who did choose to remain in the path of ever present danger have rallied around this message. A thriving underground church is multiplying in a huge area (about the size of North Korea) in the south and east of Columbia where Bibles, church buildings, formal ministry, and even house meetings have been prohibited for more than 25 years.

Severe persecution in rural Colombia has actually served to bring real Christians together in deepening Christian relationships, identify the true church, and cleanse believers from corruption. This has been possible because of the remnant that has been chosen to fight the good fight of faith.

Available where books are sold

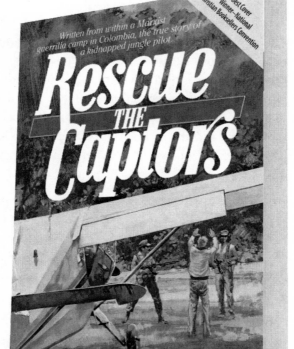

*Written from within a Marxist
guerrilla camp in Colombia, the true story of
a kidnapped jungle pilot*

Rescue
THE
Captors

Russell Stendal

Held at gunpoint deep in the jungle and with little else to occupy his time, Russell asked for some paper and began to write. He told the story of his life and kept a record of his experience in the guerrilla camp. His "book" became a bridge to the men who held him hostage and now serves as the basis for this incredible true story of how God's love penetrated a physical and ideological jungle.

I told my captors that they had two choices, either kill me, or let me go for whatever small amount my family could afford. One of the guerrillas turned and asked me if I was afraid to die. I replied that dying is obviously uncomfortable, but yes, I was prepared to die.

My captors tied me up and left the rope on day and night. They were seriously trying to completely break me psychologically and then brainwash me. Every day new things were done to alter me and work towards that goal. My captors started telling me scare stories. Some of these stories were about wild animals. They told me some of the wildest, hair-raising tales about lions and tigers that I have ever heard. These stories were designed both to intimidate me, reducing my ability to sleep, and to cause me to think twice before I decided to try to escape into the jungle again.

Available where books are sold

jubilee
B I B L E 2000

*Hear what God is
saying through this
original translation*

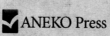

ANEKO Press

CPSIA information can be obtained at www.ICGtesting.com
Printed in the USA
LVOW10s0713070715

445169LV00006B/218/P